Women Rabbis:
Exploration & Celebration

Women Rabbis:
Exploration & Celebration

Papers Delivered at an
Academic Conference Honoring
Twenty Years of
Women in the Rabbinate

1972-1992

Edited by
Gary P. Zola

HUC-JIR Rabbinic Alumni Association Press

Cincinnati • New York • Los Angeles • Jerusalem

ISBN 0-87820-214-5

1. Women Rabbis–United States–Congresses. 2. Reform Judaism–United
State–Congresses. 3. Women in Judaism–Congresses.
I. Zola, Gary Phillip
BM652.W66   1996
296.6 ' 1 ' 082–dc20   96–25781 CIP

For
the women and men
of the
Reform rabbinate

Table of Contents ⚛️

Acknowledgments

It has been a privilege to edit the work of the learned scholars and colleagues who wrote these papers for delivery at a symposium entitled "Exploration and Celebration: Twenty Years of Women in the Rabbinate, 1972-1992." I have learned much from their research and insight.

I am indebted to my teacher and friend Dr. Alfred Gottschalk, now Chancellor of the Hebrew Union College-Jewish Institute of Religion, for his unflagging support and encouragement. During the course of his long and distinguished career at the helm of HUC-JIR, Dr. Gottschalk played a pivotal role in championing the ordination of women rabbis. In 1972 he blessed the ordination of Sally Priesand, the first woman to receive ordination from the faculty of a rabbinical seminary. Twenty years later—in 1992—Dr. Gottschalk ordained Naamah Kelman, the first woman to complete the HUC-JIR Israeli Rabbinic Program. The character of the American rabbinate has been transformed under his watch; Dr. Gottschalk oversaw the ordination of 923 rabbis between the years 1971-1995—among them 239 women. Clearly, his interest both in the symposium and in this publication of essays reflects his commitment to an ideal that literally charted the course of his professional life from its very beginnings.

Scholars who have been fortunate enough to spend time examining the treasures housed in the College-Institute's Klau Library and American

Jewish Archives know that the members of its helpful staff spare no effort in support of research. In particular, I remain ever grateful to Dr. Herbert Zafren and Dr. David Gilner of the Klau Library, and to Dr. Abraham Peck and Mr. Kevin Proffitt of the American Jewish Archives for nourishing the helpful spirit that characterizes these great repositories of learning. It is also my pleasure to acknowledge the excellent work of Mrs. Beverly Denbow, copy editor extraordinaire. This book has benefited greatly from her discerning eye.

I owe a colossal measure of debt to those who support me in my daily labors: my compatriot and friend, Ms. Lisa B. Frankel, the administrative director of the National Office of Admissions, Student Affairs, and Alumni Relations. Her able hand has literally touched every aspect of this work. For her loyal support and encouragement, I am truly grateful. Thanks are also due to Ms. Amelia Smith, secretary in the National Office of Admissions and Student Affairs, for her tireless service. Ms. Barbara Hahn, secretary in the National Office of Alumni Relations, deserves special recognition for this book's exceptionally beautiful layout and design. And, as always, I thank my dearest Stefi and my four darlings, Mandi, Jory, Jeremy, and Samantha, for their steadfast love and encouragement.

Finally, I wish to acknowledge, with admiration and respect, the indomitable work of my colleagues, the women and men of the Reform rabbinate. Day after day, they dedicate themselves anew to the task of transmitting their sense of the covenant from generation to generation. To them, this publication is affectionately dedicated.

Gary P. Zola
Cincinnati, Ohio
February 5, 1996
15 Shevat 5756

Women Rabbis:
Exploration & Celebration

Twenty Years of Women in the Rabbinate:

An Introductory Essay

Gary P. Zola

It is possible to argue that the story of how women entered the rabbinate in America may be traced back to an eleven-year-old schoolgirl named Julia Ettinger. Julia was one of the fourteen students sitting in the vestry of Cincinnati's Mound Street Temple when Hebrew Union College (HUC) opened its doors in October 1875. Despite the fact that the presence of women in the halls of HUC goes back to the school's very first days, no one believed seriously that a woman would actually enter the rabbinate. Even though Isaac Mayer Wise, the school's founder and first president, had declared publicly that he was ready and eager to educate and ordain women rabbis, no evidence exists to suggest that he ever actively sought or encouraged a woman to pursue ordination. So why was Julia in the classroom? The fledgling school needed a student body or, as one scholar put it, in order to give the new institution the dignity of a school, "the Hebrew Union College had to be drummed up." Yet, as we shall see, the road from matriculation to ordination was a long and circuitous route for the American Jewish woman.[1]

No one took seriously the idea that a woman would actually want to become a rabbi until Ray (Rachel) Frank (1864/65-1948) began attending lectures at the Hebrew Union College in January 1893. Frank, an exceedingly talented and capable woman, was a learned (though self-taught) Jew.

In 1890 she had organized the small Jewish community in Spokane, Washington, and conducted High Holy Day services. Frank worked as teacher, writer, and preacher in both Jewish and Christian pulpits throughout the West. Apparently, her oratorical skills were impressive; it is said that she received invitations to become the spiritual leader of a synagogue. Little wonder that the news of Frank's presence in the classrooms of HUC (together with a second woman—Lena Aronsohn of Little Rock, Arkansas) sparked considerable public comment. Though Frank, called the "girl rabbi of the West," never publicly declared her own desire to obtain ordination from the seminary, she insisted that women deserved the opportunity to become rabbis and lay leaders for the Jewish community.[2]

Henrietta Szold (1860-1945), the prominent founder of Hadassah, the well-known Zionist organization for women, studied at the Jewish Theological Seminary (JTS) from 1903 to 1906. Like Ray Frank, Henrietta Szold maintained that she never had any intention of pursuing ordination. Nevertheless, her presence in the classroom provoked opponents to accuse her of furtively harboring rabbinical ambition. To be sure, Henrietta—the daughter of a distinguished and modern-thinking rabbi, Benjamin Szold of Baltimore—was unquestionably up to the task. Despite the fact that Szold denied rumors that she was seeking ordination, after 1909 JTS decided to avoid the question in the future by directing women interested in pursuing higher Jewish education to enroll in its Teacher's Institute.[3]

The daughter of HUC professor David Neumark, Martha, holds the distinction of being the first documented case of a woman openly and vigorously pursuing rabbinical ordination. Martha had been a student at HUC since 1919. In 1921, the young woman asked that she be permitted to lead High Holy Day services in the fall of that year. Her request was granted. By asking for a student pulpit, Martha Neumark conveyed a determination that prompted HUC president Kaufmann Kohler to form a faculty committee to consider the feasibility of granting women rabbinic ordination. Despite the fact that a number of HUC faculty members had signed a resolution stating that rabbinical ordination should not be denied women, Neumark's request was ultimately blocked by the laity; the school's board of governors voted in 1923 "that no change should be made in the present practice of limiting to males the right...of entering the rabbinate."[4]

If Neumark was the first woman to formally seek rabbinic ordination, Irma Levy Lindheim (1886-1978) was the first to be granted permission to enroll in a rabbinical course of study. A protégée of Henrietta Szold, Lindheim was eager to enhance her limited reservoir of Jewish knowledge. As a result of a chance meeting with Stephen S. Wise, founder and president of the newly established Jewish Institute of Religion (JIR), Lindheim decided in 1922 to enroll in JIR. A capable and enthusiastic student, Lindheim's hunger for Jewish learning intensified after matriculation. In 1923 she asked the school's faculty to admit her to the regular course of rabbinical study. Though the faculty initially demurred, Lindheim was indeed given permission to begin her studies later the same year.

Unfortunately, complications in her personal life ultimately forced Irma to withdraw from the program one year prior to the time of her anticipated ordination. Years later, Lindheim wrote that she hoped her initiatives would serve as a precedent for women who would come after her: "I had [no] plan to function as a rabbi. I simply believed that...if I prepared myself in accordance with the requirements of being a rabbi, the door would be opened for other women, should they wish and have the gift to minister to congregations."[5]

Lindheim's wishes aside, her years at JIR did not pave the way for another woman who hoped to attain rabbinical ordination: Helen Hadassah Levinthal (1910-1989). In contrast to Irma Lindheim, Helen (daughter of the distinguished Conservative rabbi Israel Levinthal) actually completed all of JIR's requirements for ordination. The faculty discussed the prospect of Helen's ordination in earnest but, in the end, she was not ordained. To recognize her academic achievements, however, Levinthal was given a teaching certificate and a master's degree in Hebrew literature.[6]

And so it went throughout the first half of the twentieth century. Despite Reform Judaism's growing public commitment to women's equality, Jewish women with a desire to learn and lead were able to advance only so far. Though she was not a North American, Lily Montagu (1873-1963), a distinguished founder of the Liberal Jewish movement in Great Britain, deserves mention in any discussion relating to women in the rabbinate. Montagu led worship services regularly and was a highly regarded preacher during the first half of the twentieth century. Her achievements were remarkable indeed, and though she was a social worker and magistrate by profession, there can be little doubt that her extraordinary career in Jewish communal life blazed a trail for the women rabbis who arose a generation later. There were also North American women like Carrie Simon (1872-1961), Jennie Purvin (1873-1958), and Hannah G. Solomon (1858-1942), who devoted their lives to the development of a wide array of Jewish women's organizations and women's auxiliary groups in synagogues. During the first decades of the twentieth century, dozens of women studied in the classrooms of HUC, JIR, and JTS. Many took classes along with male rabbinic students. It is impossible to ascertain how many of these women actually yearned privately to become rabbis. No doubt—either consciously or unconsciously—many of them did. Nevertheless, these women faced the same barriers that confronted all American career women during the first half of the twentieth century: Though professional opportunities were expanding, aspiring women faced an impenetrable wall of prejudices that effectively kept them at bay.[7]

Considering the remarkable number of Jewish women in America who expressed their desire to enter the rabbinate, it is interesting to note that the first female rabbi in modern Jewish history was a young German woman—Regina Jonas (1902-44) of Berlin. Jonas studied at the Hochschule für die Wissenschaft des Judentums, a liberal rabbinic seminary that began permitting women to enroll in courses of study in the mid-1920s. Jonas earned the title of Akademische Religionslehrerin (Academic Teacher of Religion) in 1930. In partial fulfillment of the requirements for this degree, Jonas wrote a halakhic thesis entitled: "Can a Woman Hold Rabbinical Office?" In her introduction to this work, Jonas wrote that she undertook the study because she hoped to enter the rabbinate "when that will be possible."[8]

While still at the seminary, Jonas enrolled in courses that would prepare her for a career in the rabbinate. The Hochschule provided Jonas with a codicil to her transcript certifying she had "participated in the homiletic exercises with great success, and showed herself a thoughtful, skilled preacher." Despite these successes, Jonas left school without ordination. She worked exclusively as a teacher after graduation, but in 1935 Rabbi Max Dienemann, the liberal rabbi of Offenbach, examined Jonas and provided her with a rabbinic diploma (*Hattarat Hora'ah*) verifying her competence to hold "rabbinical office." It was, ironically, Nazi brutality that made it possible for Jonas to begin functioning as a rabbi. As the German Jewry endured the bewildering effects of rampant isolation, oppression, and dissolution, the community's religious/spiritual needs intensified. The administration of the Jewish community employed Jonas in 1937 and authorized her to "carry out rabbinic-spiritual care." Jonas's rabbinical role continued to increase as institutional order collapsed. She served her people heroically to the very end, ministering and teaching for two years in the Terézin concentration camp. In late October 1944, Rabbi Jonas died in Auschwitz.[9]

In 1972, twenty-eight years after Jonas's death, nearly one hundred years after Julia Ettinger studied with Isaac Mayer Wise, and fifty years after the HUC faculty formally agreed to ordain women rabbis, the historic distinction of becoming the first woman in Jewish history to receive ordination from the faculty of a rabbinical seminary came to Sally Jane Priesand, a twenty-six-year old woman from Cleveland, Ohio.[10]

What were the sociological, economic, and historic factors that made it feasible for this watershed event to occur in the early 1970s? Even Rabbi Priesand herself cannot say for sure why she was the one who ultimately became *the first woman rabbi* as opposed to one of the many women trailblazers who preceded her or who followed closely behind. Some contend that the primary catalytic factor was the emergence of the modern feminist movement.[11] Others point to the antiestablishment/counterculture spirit that typified the late 1960s and early 1970s. Undoubtedly, an accurate explanation will ultimately derive from a confluence of factors. We know one thing for certain: There is still much more we can learn about this prefatory period in the history of women in the rabbinate.[12]

Considering, though, how long it took for women to enter the rabbinate, the degree to which women have flourished in the American rabbinate over that past twenty years is nothing short of phenomenal. Today, women constitute one-half of the student body in the Rabbinic School of the Hebrew Union College-Jewish Institute of Religion, and practically one-fourth of HUC-JIR's nonretired alumni are women. This same trend informs the demography of the other non-Orthodox movements in Judaism: One-half the student body of the Reconstructionist Rabbinical College (RRC) and approximately one-third of the student body of Conservative Judaism's Jewish Theological Seminary (which ordained its first woman rabbi in 1985, more than a decade after the Reform movement did so) are women. Within the brief span of one-score years, women have not merely "entered" the non-Orthodox rabbinate, they have, quite literally, assumed a substantive segment of this calling's population.[13]

Remarkable though these figures may be, statistics alone cannot adequately describe women's experiences during their years in the rabbinate. For women rabbis, success and struggle go hand in hand. As *Ms.* magazine observed in 1982, "When Sally Priesand was ordained as the first woman rabbi, her challenges weren't over."[14]

Over the years, observers expressed doubt about women's commitment to the rabbinate as a profession. Some speculation has suggested women would abandon the rabbinate just as soon as they found a husband and began to raise a family. Others predicted that many (if not most) congregations would simply refuse to hire women rabbis. And there were some who wondered whether women would actually remain in the ministry once they had experienced the career's demanding rigors. These voices of apprehension and skepticism have been discredited by real life experience. We know, however, that women rabbis have faced, and undoubtedly will continue to face, daunting professional challenges. Very little has been written about these struggles and strains to date. The few impressionistic accounts that do exist attest to the fact that, twenty-some years after Rabbi Priesand's ordination, women rabbis still face a wide variety of obstacles that hinder their career paths.[15]

Yet women rabbis have contributed mightily to Jewish life in North America—even though they have unquestionably endured professional hardships and adversity. The significance of their contributions can scarcely be exaggerated. First, women rabbis have affected the fundamental nature of contemporary Jewish ritual, liturgy, and theology. Since the 1970s, there has been a tremendous outpouring of spiritual literature written by and for women. Simultaneously, women have been responsible for establishing an array of new communal organizations like Ezrat Nashim (1971), a study and feminist consciousness-raising group, and the Jewish Feminist Organization (1974), whose purpose was to pursue "full, direct and equal participation of women at all levels of Jewish life." Women rabbis have also contributed to the development of feminist journals, women's *chavurot* (worship circles), and a variety of innovative life-cycle ceremonies. At the same time, women rabbis have been advocates for overhauling the entrenched, male-dominated political structures that have long typified so many segments of Jewish life.[16]

Radical transformations have occurred over the past two decades—and are *still* occurring—with such tremendous velocity that we have scarcely had time to reflect on the meaning of these extraordinary developments. Although the growth of women's studies as an academic discipline has led to the appearance of new studies on women in Judaism and the lives of individual Jewish women, few recent works have focused intently on the lives and experiences of women rabbis. Recently, the women rabbis of Great Britain have begun the process of addressing this lacuna by publishing an intriguing collection of their own stories and personal reflections. In addition, there have been a few initial sociological studies that have attempted to analyze the professional contributions of women rabbis. The tentative findings indicate that women rabbis believe they are more approachable and less formal than their male counterparts. They also believe that they are more likely to "personalize" religious ceremonies and that their preaching style is more emotional and relational than that of their male colleagues.[17]

What have women rabbis contributed to their profession and, of equal importance, how has the existence of women rabbis affected the self-identity of Jewish women, Jewish men, and Jewish religious life? It is hoped that—considered together—the essays in this volume will begin to address, preliminarily, these questions. All of these essays were originally presented at an academic conference entitled "Exploration and Celebration: An Academic Symposium Honoring the Twentieth Anniversary of Women in the Rabbinate." This unique symposium was jointly sponsored by the HUC-JIR Rabbinic Alumni Association and the National Federation of Temple Sisterhoods-Women of Reform Judaism. Several hundred individuals—HUC-JIR alumni, rabbis from other movements, academicians, and interested laypersons—attended this conference, which was held at the New York campus of the Hebrew Union College-Jewish Institute of Religion on January 30-31, 1993. The essays were written specifically for this colloquium by distinguished scholars and rabbis. They appear in this volume in the order they were delivered—organized in three sections that correspond to the three overarching questions that framed the symposium itself:

I.   **HOW DID WE REACH THIS ANNIVERSARY**? What has been the history of women's journey to ordination? How has this history changed and challenged Reform Judaism and the larger Jewish community?

In her essay, Ellen M. Umansky draws upon her pioneering research into the history of women in the rabbinate and catalogues the names of those who paved the way toward the ordination of women. Umansky's historical reconstruction lends support to the contention that Reform Judaism's long-standing commitment to religious equality for women was in reality "a logical consequence of [its] ideology, not a central cause." Religious equality for women would become a top priority only when women themselves began to unify and press for change. By means of comparison and contrast, Jonathan D. Sarna's resourceful essay on the career of Antoinette Brown Blackwell, the first ordained female minister in the United States, broadens our understanding of the path that led to the ordination of women rabbis. Sarna points out that the vocational challenges women rabbis are facing today are clearly not without historical precedent. The story of Brown Blackwell's career in the ministry informs us that professional doubts, spiritual challenges, and tensions that often polarize family and career are not unique to women in the rabbinate. To the contrary, these issues constitute conflicts with which women clergy have been grappling for quite some time.

Brown Blackwell's ordination came 119 years before that of Sally Priesand. For Sarna, this fact reminds us that in responding to new social realities, Judaism—indeed Reform Judaism—transforms itself more hesitantly than many other religious traditions because Jewish practice is so intensely rooted in law and venerated traditions. Finally, Sarna argues that the actuality of ordination for women—from Antoinette Brown Blackwell to Sally Priesand and beyond—represents an act of what is today called "radical empowerment," an entitlement that ultimately serves to liberate Jewish women from premodern shackles that constrained them well into the twentieth century.

II. **WHERE ARE WE NOW AS WE MARK THIS ANNIVERSARY?**
How has the presence of women rabbis changed and challenged Reform Jewish liturgy, theology, and Jewish communal leadership?

In assuming the tasks that have long been reserved exclusively for the male sphere, women have faced another crucial challenge that modernity poses for Jews and Judaism: the quest for spiritual meaning and fulfillment in the modern world. Alienation and estrangement are common features of contemporary society. Many Jewish women struggle with this spiritual void when they encounter a Judaism fraught with male-defined liturgy and theology. This state has been termed by some scholars as woman's "alterity"—the problematics of women's pervasive absence in Jewish lore and literature. As spiritual leaders and religious teachers, women rabbis frequently find themselves on the front line in our contemporary search for religious meaning.

Amplifying on his ground-breaking work in this field, Howard Eilberg-Schwartz explores the dilemmas created by the concept of God's maleness for both men and women today. He suggests that a new approach to theological reflection may enable men to recognize their need for "loving images of a male father figure" just as women have need for a loving image of a female mother figure. Acknowledging the potential danger in deifying masculinity, Eilberg-Schwartz intriguingly asserts that women and men may have assumed, mistakenly, that they already fully understood what Judaism has to say about masculinity.

Rabbi Laura Geller's essay is an incisive analysis of the current state of women in positions of Jewish leadership. Geller, one of the first women ordained by HUC-JIR, has had a truly remarkable rabbinate serving on the college campus, in Jewish organizational life, and in the congregation. Rabbi Geller describes the dramatic strides women like herself have made in the rabbinate, cantorate, as well as in other leadership positions. The gains have been impressive, but they come at a high price. Geller reminds us that if the strides women rabbis have made to date are to have enduring value, then the total character of Jewish institutional life must be transformed in the years ahead.

III. **ON THE BASIS OF THE PAST AND THE PRESENT, WHAT CAN WE EXPECT FROM THE FUTURE?** How will women rabbis affect the future of the rabbinate, congregational life, and Jewish communal life as we enter the twenty-first century?

The contention that men and women perceive life's experiences differently constitutes something of a double-edged sword. On the one hand, the notion that women are spiritually distinct from men has been used (from the distant past up through our own day) to justify the exclusion of women from a variety of cultural spheres. On the other hand, the effect of Carol Gilligan's influential analysis, *In a Different Voice*, has been felt in the rabbinate as in the clergy in general. Many have argued that, as a consequence of their sexual essence, men and women rabbis function differently: They rely on different styles of interrelating (hierarchical versus relational), they employ distinct approaches to preaching (exhortative versus affective), and they use discrete modes of language (authoritative versus inclusive). Others contend that the differences in "male/female" styles of ministry are not nearly as consequential as some have asserted.[18]

Women rabbis are especially familiar with the tension that impels them to maintain the most meaningful components of Jewish tradition while, simultaneously, working to transform Judaism's oppressive elements. Basing her ideas on the theory that men and women have distinct styles of spiritual communication, Rabbi Elyse Frishman proposes a radical reexamination of the meaning of halakhah in Judaism. Frishman suggests that the traditional halakhah we have inherited is a male-oriented "mitzvah system"—an authoritative, hierarchical system of directives. Revitalizing the Jewish future, Rabbi Frishman opines, will necessitate that Reform Judaism jettison the male-oriented halakhah in favor of a female-oriented relational covenant. In order for rabbis to safeguard Judaism's spiritual heritage for another generation, Frishman urges a female-oriented approach to halakhah—one that depends upon the emotional/spiritual bond, not the divine command.[19]

Affirming the importance of a distinct feminist approach to Judaism, Professor David Ellenson also argues that a relational, nonhierarchical approach to Judaism is consistent with the fundamental thrust of the biblical and rabbinic tradition. Ellenson envisions a future in which Jewish spirituality and Jewish communal structure will be influenced by a feminist ethos that embodies the tradition's most noble sentiments: compassion, caring, and relationships.

Rabbi Nancy Fuchs-Kreimer offers us a slightly "different view of difference," suggesting that the very presence of women in the rabbinate proves diversity and variation are at the heart of the Jewish experience. As a byproduct of this affirmation, Fuchs-Kreimer envisions a future that is permeated with Jewish choices. God, religious leaders, and Jewish people will be celebrated in variety. This heterogeneity will, in turn, foster a spirit of cooperation and shared experience.

Finally, the collection of articles begins and concludes, appropriately, with remarks by Dr. Alfred Gottschalk, now Chancellor of the Hebrew Union College-Jewish Institute of Religion, and Rabbi Sally J. Priesand. On June 3, 1972, in the historic Isaac M. Wise (Plum Street) Temple in Cincinnati, these two individuals took center stage to fulfill their destiny in a momentous, landmark ceremony that marked the first time in history that a rabbinical seminary conferred ordination on a woman. Neither Gottschalk nor Priesand had anticipated facing one another on that Shabbat morning. Priesand was less than two years from her anticipated date of ordination when Nelson Glueck, the College-Institute's President, died on February 12, 1971. The delicate task of navigating the institution's final steps on the road toward Sally's ordination were taken by its new leader,

Alfred Gottschalk. From that point on, their respective rabbinical careers would be influenced by the impact of this historic encounter. Students of women and religion will undoubtedly value the personal reflections of these two distinguished rabbis who, twenty years ago, became agents of history.

The spirit of the essays collected in this volume truly epitomizes the focus of the academic symposium for which they were originally commissioned. Considered together, they constitute a unique blend of scholarship and ceremony, exploration and celebration. It is hoped that this collection will serve as a springboard for future research into the modern Jewish woman and her unfolding role in the contemporary world of Jewish thought and practice.

Notes

1. For quote, see Sefton D. Temkin, *Isaac Mayer Wise: Shaping American Judaism* (New York: Oxford University Press, 1992), 272. On the push to ordain women, see especially Ellen M. Umansky, "Women in Judaism: From the Reform Movement to Contemporary Jewish Religious Feminism," in *Women of Spirit: Female Leadership in the Jewish and Christian Traditions*, edited by Rosemary Radford Ruether and Eleanor Mclaughlin (New York: Simon and Schuster, 1979), 301-32. See also Pamela S. Nadell, "The Women Who Would Be Rabbis," in *Gender and Judaism*, edited by T. M. Rudavsky (New York: New York University Press, 1995), 123-34; and Ellen M. Umansky, "Spiritual Expressions: Jewish Women's Religious Lives in the Twentieth-Century United States," in *Jewish Women in Historical Perspective*, edited by Judith R. Baskin (Detroit: Wayne State University Press, 1991), 265-88. See also Jacob Rader Marcus, *The American Jewish Woman, 1654-1980* (Cincinnati: Ktav, 1981), 76-9.

2. For insight into Frank's view on women in the rabbinate, see Jacob Rader Marcus, *The American Jewish Woman: A Documentary History* (New York: Ktav, 1981), 380-83. On Ray Frank's career, see Reva Clar and William M. Kramer, "The Girl Rabbi of the Golden West: The Adventurous Life of Ray Frank in Nevada, California and the Northwest," *Western States Jewish History* 18 (1986): 99-111, 223-36, 336-51. According to Clar and Kramer, Lena Aronsohn came to HUC with the expressed desire of becoming a rabbi. See also Marcus, *American Jewish Woman, 1654-1980*, 78-9 and Nadell, "Women Who Would Be Rabbis," 126.

3. On Szold's years at JTS see Nadell, "Women Who Would Be Rabbis," 125-6; Robert Gordis, "The Ordination of Women—A History of the Question," *Judaism* 33 (Winter 1984): 7, and Marcus, *American Jewish Woman, 1654-1980*, 93.

4.   For quote, see Michael A. Meyer, *Hebrew Union College-Jewish Institute of Religion: A Centennial History*, rev. ed., edited by Gary P. Zola, (Cincinnati: Hebrew Union College Press, 1992), 99. On Martha Neumark, see Umansky, "Women in Judaism," 339-41; idem., "Spiritual Expressions," 278-80.

5.   For quote, see Nadell, "Women Who Would Be Rabbis," 129. On Lindheim, see especially Marcus, *American Jewish Woman: A Documentary History*, 329-34, 714-20; and Linda Gordon Kuzmack, *The Emergence of the Jewish Woman's Movement in England and the United States, 1881-1933* (Columbus: Ohio State University Press, 1990), chap. 7.

6.   On Levinthal, see Kuzmack, *Emergence of the Jewish Woman's Movement*, and Umansky, "Women in Judaism," 341. Existing documentation does not disclose the actual reason Levinthal did not receive her ordination despite the fact that she had successfully completed the required course work. It has been suggested that the JIR faculty voted furtively not to ordain Ms. Levinthal.   Others speculate that Stephen Wise may have eschewed ordaining Levinthal in deference to the religious sensibilities of the more traditionally-minded Israel H. Levinthal (1888-1982), Wise's close friend.

7.   On the impediments facing women who tried to enter professions, see Penina Migdal Glazer and Miriam Slater, *Unequal Colleagues: The Entrance of Women into the Professions, 1890-1940* (New Brunswick: Rutgers University Press, 1987), 14; and Mary Roth Walsh, *"Doctors Wanted: No Women Need Apply"; Sexual Barriers in the Medical Profession, 1835-1975* (New Haven: Yale University Press, 1977). On Lily Montagu, see Ellen M. Umansky, *Lily Montagu and the Advancement of Liberal Judaism: From Vision to Vocation* (Lewiston, New York: Edwin Mellen Press, 1983). Regarding women of the National Federation of Temple Sisterhoods, the Women's League of the United Synagogue, the National Council of Jewish Women, and other such organizations, see Marcus, *American Jewish Woman: A Documentary History*, passim. Dozens of women earned baccalaureate degrees in Hebrew letters or education degrees from HUC, JIR, and JTS's Teacher's Institute. We may never know how many of these ambitious young women would have entered the rabbinate had they been permitted to do so. Though Pamela S. Nadell and Ellen M. Umansky have identified a number of these heretofore unsung trailblazers, there are, undoubtedly, many others (women like Avis

Shulman and Dora Askowith) whose story has—as of yet—not been chronicled.

8. For the most recent article, and the most important to date, on Regina Jonas, see Katharina von Kellenbach, "'God Does Not Oppress Any Human Being': The Life and Thought of Rabbi Regina Jonas," *Leo Baeck Institute Year Book* 39 (1994): 213-25. On the Hochschule, see Richard Fuchs, "The 'Hochshule für die Wissenschaft des Judentums' in the Period of Nazi Rule," *Leo Baeck Institute Year Book* 12 (1967), 3-31.

9. Von Kellenbach, "'God Does Not Oppress,'" 221-24. On Jonas, see also Alexander Guttmann, "The Woman Rabbi: A Historical Perspective," *Journal of Reform Judaism* 24 (Summer 1982) 3: 21-5; and Marcus, *American Jewish Woman, A Documentary History*, 889.

10. On Sally Priesand's ordination, see Michael A. Meyer, *Response to Modernity: A History of the Reform Movement in Judaism* (New York: Oxford University Press, 1988), 379-80; and Marcus, *American Jewish Woman, A Documentary History*, 887-93.

11. Jacob Rader Marcus points out that present-day historians cite Betty Friedan's *Feminine Mystique*, first published in 1963, and the founding of the National Organization for Women in 1966 as milestones in the modern reawakening of the women's liberation movement. See Marcus, *American Jewish Woman, 1654-1980*, 149-56. It seems unlikely that the feminist movement per se influenced Sally Priesand, whose own reminiscences suggest that in the mid-1960's she herself was not particularly aware of the feminist stirrings. Rabbi Priesand described her decision to become a rabbi as "an affirmation of my belief in God, in the worth of each individual, and in Judaism as a way of life." See Sally J. Priesand, *Judaism and the New Woman* (New York: Behrman House, 1975), preface.

12. See Priesand, *Judaism and the New Woman*, preface. With regard to factors contributing to Sally Priesand's ordination, some believe that Nelson Glueck's resolve to ordain women rabbis may be attributed to the fact that his wife, Helen Glueck, M.D., distinguished herself as a hematologist at a time when medicine was an extremely inhospitable career for women. Years later, Rabbi Priesand remembered that Dr. Glueck was "a particular source of strength."

13. The faculty of the Jewish Theological Seminary voted in favor of ordaining women on October 24, 1983. JTS ordained Amy Eilberg in May 1985. For a history of events leading up to JTS's decision to ordain women, see especially Marilyn G. Thorne, "The Ordination of Women Rabbis" (master's thesis, San Francisco State University, 1990); and Simon Greenberg, ed., *The Ordination of Women Rabbis* (New York: Jewish Theological Seminary, 1988). For a comparative look at the history of women's ordination in Reform and Conservative Judaism, see Gary P. Zola, "HUC, JTS, and Women Rabbis," *Journal of Reform Judaism* 31 (Fall 1984).

14. As quoted in Joanne Wolf Shank, "Women in the Rabbinate: New Paths and New Truths" (master's thesis, Smith College, 1985).

15. Sally Priesand recalled that "many believed I was studying at HUC-JIR to beome a *rebbetzin* rather than a rabbi, to marry rather than to officiate." See Priesand, *Judaism and the New Woman*, preface. Regarding congregations rejecting women rabbis, see ibid. and see David Novak, "Women in the Rabbinate?" *Judaism* 33 (Winter 1984): 53. For a helpful overview on theories relating to the prospect of women's endurance in the clergy, see Shenk, "Women in the Rabbinate," 26 and chap. 2. See also Judith A. Bluestein, "Women Rabbis: A Study of Advancement," typescript, 1983, American Jewish Archives, and Rachel Susan Frielich, "A Sociological Analysis of the Ordination of Women as Conservative Rabbis," (bachelor's thesis, Barnard College, 1984); Task Force on the Equality of Women in Judaism, *Choosing a New Rabbi: The Impact of Female Rabbinic Candidates on the Placement Process* (Paramus, N.J.; New Jersey-West Hudson Valley Council of the Union of American Hebrew Congregations, 1987); and Elaine Shizhal Cohen, "Rabbis' Roles and Occupational Goals: Men and Women in the Contemporary American Rabbinate," *Conservative Judaism* 42 (Fall 1989): 20-30.

16. For quote, see Umansky, "Women in Judaism," 347. Professor Umansky has recently composed a helpful bibliographical essay: "Critical Studies of Women in Jewish Life: Some Recent Works," *CCAR Journal* 34 (Spring 1992): 1-15. On Ezrat Nashim, the Jewish Feminist Organization,

see Alan Silverstein, "The Evolution of Ezrat Nashim," *Conservative Judaism* 30 (Fall 1975): 41-51. On Ezrat Nashim and other trailblazing organizations, see Umansky, "Women in Judaism," 346-50. For an impressive sampling of the variety of women's spiritual strivings in the contemporary period, see ibid. and see Ellen M. Umansky and Diane Ashton, eds., *Four Centuries of Jewish Women's Spirituality: A Sourcebook* (Boston: Beacon Press, 1992), 191-334.

17. Sybil Sheridan, ed., *Hear Our Voice: Women Rabbis Tell Their Stories* (London: SCM Press, 1994). One of the best studies on the background, motivation, and experiences of women rabbis is Rita J. Simon, "Rabbis and Ministers: Women of the Book and the Cloth," in *Rabbis, Lawyers, Immigrants, Thieves: Exploring Women's Roles* (Westport, Conn.: Praeger, 1993), 63-71. See also Janet Marder, "How Women Are Changing the Rabbinate," *Reform Judaism* (Summer 1991): 4-8.

18. Carol Gilligan, *In a Different Voice* (Cambridge: Harvard University Press, 1982). For an alternative view, see Edward C. Lehman, Jr., "Gender and Ministry Style: Things Not What They Seem?" in *Gender and Religion*, edited by William H. Swatos, Jr. (New Brunswick, N.J.: Transaction Publishers, 1994), 3-13.

19. Reena Sigman Friedman reports that opponents to the ordination of women rabbis within Conservative Judaism feared that women rabbis would contribute to the decline of *halakhah's* authority and encourage defections from halakhic Judaism. See her "The Politics of Women's Ordination," *Lilith* 6 (June 1979): 9.

"Who Shall Sojourn in the Tabernacle…":

Celebrating Twenty Years of Women in the Rabbinate

Alfred Gottschalk

It is with a tremendous sense of celebration that I welcome you to this auspicious gathering, "Exploration and Celebration: Twenty Years of Women in the Rabbinate." Distinguished alumnae, colleagues from the Conservative and Reconstructionist movements, scholars and friends have gathered together from across North America to mark this special anniversary and to participate in this, the *first* academic exploration of the historic significance of twenty years of women in the rabbinate–for women, for Reform Judaism, and for the Jewish people.

This historic development in the modernization of American religious leadership fulfilled the vision of our school's founders, Rabbi Isaac Mayer Wise and Rabbi Stephen S. Wise. When the Hebrew Union College opened its doors in 1875 in Cincinnati, Ohio, Rabbi Isaac Mayer Wise welcomed to its first class of sixteen freshmen a woman named Julia Ettinger. When Rabbi Stephen S. Wise established the New York-based Jewish Institute of Religion in 1922, women were included in the student body. Our founders hoped that the rabbinic leadership of American Jewry would transmit the prophetic tradition of our faith through a progressive conception of Judaism reflective of and responsive to the needs of living in modernity. It is a fundamental reality of modern society that women are equal citizens in every respect and therefore entitled to equal rights, equal opportunity, and equal responsibility.

It was twenty years ago that I had the distinct privilege of ordaining Rabbi Sally J. Priesand as the first woman rabbi in America. I will never forget that day. Sally and I stood together before the open Ark at the historic Plum Street Temple in Cincinnati. As I ordained Sally, thoughts of all who made this historical moment possible flooded my mind. After I finished reciting the words of the priestly blessing, Sally descended from the bimah in order to return to her seat. At that moment, all of her classmates spontaneously rose from their seats and offered their sustained applause. All present felt the significance of that remarkable moment.

The ordination of Rabbi Priesand cleared the way for a long overdue empowerment of women in Reform Judaism and the Jewish clergy. Our recognition of the equality of women in Jewish life led eventually to the ordination of women rabbis at the Reconstructionist and Conservative seminaries. Sally's ordination also was a paradigm for the investiture of women cantors at the Hebrew Union College-Jewish Institute of Religion some years later. Subsequently the Jewish Theological Seminary also recognized the role of women as *shelichei tzibbur* (prayer leaders).

Facts and figures bespeak the dramatic changes that have occurred in these intervening years and are helpful in gauging our progress:

◊ As of January 31, 1993, the College-Institute had ordained 187 Reform women rabbis, and women currently make up 47 percent of the students in the rabbinic program.

◊ Women were admitted to our School of Sacred Music in 1971, and the first woman cantor was invested in 1975. Eighty-one women cantors have been invested to date, and the overwhelming majority of students (70 percent) in our cantorial program are women.

◊ Women now comprise one-third of our student body in our schools of graduate studies.

◊ Eighty-four percent of the students in our graduate programs of education are women.

◊ Seventy-six percent of the students in our Jewish communal service programs are women.

⬧ The classes admitted in 1992-93 for rabbinic, cantorial, education, communal service, and graduate study programs are the largest in more than a decade; the number of applicants to these programs has been increasing each year; and more and more qualified, motivated, and talented women are opting for religious leadership, especially in the fields of Jewish education and communal service.

⬧ Finally, the highlight of this twentieth anniversary year was yet another historic ordination—the ordination of Rabbi Naamah Kelman as the first woman to become a rabbi in the state of Israel. She, among the eleven alumni of the Israeli Rabbinic Program and the twelve students, two of whom are women, currently in the program, will contribute to the growth of our movement in Israel. Their ordination underscores our school's commitment to the furthering of pluralism and liberal Jewish values in Israel. We look forward to ordaining Maia Leibovic as our second woman rabbi for the Israel Progressive Movement in Jerusalem this July.[§] Our actions have impelled the Masorati movement, the conservative movement in Israel, to ordain its first woman rabbi this year.

Today, our alumnae serve congregations, large and small, throughout North America. Our alumnae reinforce Jewish identity for college youth as Hillel directors and rabbis on campuses across the country. They inspire our communal and educational centers and agencies toward innovation and creativity in outreach to the unaffiliated and the interfaith family. They provide chaplaincy for the military, hospitals and homes for the aged. They help provide relief for the hungry, the homeless, and the afflicted. Woman are also an integral part of the College-Institute's academic programs and are at the forefront of the Reform clergy and Jewish professional leadership for the twenty-first century.

We are gratified and, yes, even proud of the fact that the College-Institute has been in the vanguard advancing women's rights within Judaism:

⬧ promoting gender-free language in our prayerbooks

[§] Maia Leibovic was ordained in July 1993

◊ advocating equal opportunity for placement and employment in Reform congregations
◊ enhancing women's access to all leadership roles in the synagogue and in Jewish communal agencies
◊ adapting our liturgy for the female presence and voice
◊ supporting our alumnae with continuing education and programs for spiritual renewal
◊ establishing early childhood centers on our Cincinnati and Jerusalem campuses to provide child-care options for our students with families
◊ adding a new perspective to Jewish scholarship
◊ enhancing the egalitarian and inclusive quality of Jewish life.

Simultaneously, we are cognizant of the challenges that are still ahead. I am committed to building a strong female faculty at the College-Institute. Our student body must have the opportunity to study with outstanding female scholars—women who will serve as mentors for the coming generations. We also need to strengthen our institution's endowment resources in order to support student scholarships and fellowships, so that all of our students, men and women alike, can be more amply supported in their training to serve the Jewish people.

There is much more work to be done in our movement. We must work together so that women can break through the glass ceiling in the area of career advancement. We also need to increase the number of women who serve on the governing bodies of our school and in our movement.

These challenges will be addressed during the course of this conference's colloquia and workshops, which will analyze past trends and consider future directions in Reform Judaism, the larger Jewish community, congregational life, liturgy, theology, and leadership. I am most grateful to the leaders of our Rabbinic Alumni Association, and I am grateful to the National Federation of Temple Sisterhoods for cosponsoring this unique event with the College-Institute.

In closing, I would like to once again underscore what we know to be true in Judaism. In our faith there is an implicit egalitarian principle that sees men and women as equal partners in the service of God. On behalf of the College-Institute, I extend our enormous gratitude to the women of

Judaism who, with commitment and vitality, are fulfilling the psalmist's profound inquiry:

"Who shall sojourn in your tabernacle; who shall dwell upon your holy mountain? One who walks uprightly, works righteousness, and speaks truth in the heart."

You are all truly *n'shei chayil*—women of valor. Carry us forward into the next millennium!

A Historical Perspective

Women's Journey toward Rabbinic Ordination

Ellen M. Umansky

Approximately 150 years ago in Germany, a group of "like-thinking, progressive" rabbis convened a series of rabbinical conferences through which the ideology of the then nascent Reform movement slowly began to take shape. Among the issues discussed was the role of women in Jewish religious life. By 1846, at a conference held in Breslau, a special commission appointed to reevaluate women's traditional roles recommended that the conference declare women to be "entitled to the same religious rights and subject to the same religious duties" as men. No formal vote was taken, yet apparently no objections were raised to David Einhorn's pronouncement that it was nothing less than their "sacred duty" as Reform rabbis "to declare with all emphasis" the complete religious equality of men and women.[1]

Writing his history of the Reform movement in 1907, American reform rabbi David Philipson concluded that while the commission's report was neither discussed nor voted upon, "in practice" the commission's various recommendations as to how women's equality might best be achieved "have been carried out in reform congregations notably in the United States."[2] As evidence, Philipson pointed to the abolition of a separate women's gallery in the synagogue and the introduction of mixed seating in 1851 by Isaac Mayer Wise in Albany, New York. In his prayerbook, *Minhag America*, originally published in 1857 and revised in 1872, Wise went so far as to describe the minyan as comprising "ten adults, males or females."[3]

Similarly, Kaufmann Kohler, later to become president of Hebrew Union College, told members of the Central Conference of American Rabbis (CCAR), gathered at the historic Pittsburgh convention of 1885, that "Reform Judaism will never reach its higher goal [of spiritual and moral elevation] without having first accorded to the congregational council and in the entire religious and moral sphere of life, equal voice to woman with man."[4]

Yet as Riv-Ellen Prell has pointed out, Classical Reform's commitment to women's equality was more theoretical than real. Prell observed:

> The Reformers' concern for women was an inevitable outgrowth of their commitment to the Enlightenment's values of equality, reason, and humanism. That the role of women in Judaism was not actively addressed until the last decade of feminist activism in America, despite its prominence in Reform's initial program, is as much because social reality lags behind ideology as it is because the women's issue for Reformers was a logical consequence of their ideology, not a central cause.[5]

My own research on the roles and status of women in Reform Judaism bears out Prell's assessment. Despite early pronouncements of commitments to women's equality in Germany and later in the United States, not until the early 1960s, and even more so in the 1970s, as the burgeoning feminist movement began to create new expectations among women themselves, did women in Reform Judaism begin to press for and achieve significant change.

Hebrew Union College (HUC) opened its doors in fall 1875 to a group of nine, later sixteen, boys ages thirteen to seventeen. According to Jacob Marcus, an eleven-year-old girl was a member of the first class as well.[6] Offering an eight-year program, the first four years of which were spent studying for two hours a day with Isaac Mayer Wise and his assistant while also attending a local high school, HUC, according to Michael Meyer, "amounted to little more than an intensive religious school."[7] Thus, one should not overestimate the significance of Isaac Mayer Wise's encouraging women to attend the College. Even if he encouraged them to seek ordination (and no clear evidence exists to suggest that he did), it apparently was the board of governors, not Wise, who possessed the power to make such decisions.[8] One wonders, however, whether the two women who had earned a bachelor of Hebrew letters degree from HUC by 1900 might not have sought ordination had such an option been available to them. One wonders, too, what motivated Wise in 1892 to invite the well-known journalist and preacher, Ray Frank, to undertake theological studies at the College.

By the time she entered HUC in spring 1893, Ray Frank had already gained both national and international renown as a "lady preacher" or–as she more frequently, though erroneously, was labeled–"lady rabbi." She first came to public prominence in fall 1890, when, on the eve of Rosh Hashanah, she happened to be in Spokane, Washington (then known as Spokane Falls). Interested in attending religious services, she asked a Jewish member of the community, to whom she had letters of introduction, where services were being held. After learning that none had been planned because the number of Jews in Spokane Falls was quite small and divided by religious dissension, she offered to preach at such a service if a minyan could be gathered. At her initiative, a special edition of the *Spokane Falls Gazette* was printed announcing that a young woman would be preaching to the Jews of the community at the opera house that evening.

Returning to preach on Yom Kippur, Frank appealed to her coreligionists to resolve their differences and form themselves into a permanent congregation. They soon agreed to do so. Encouraged by her success, she spent much of the early 1890s traveling up and down the Pacific coast, establishing a number of Jewish congregations and healing congregational squabbles. By all accounts, one could describe Ray Frank as a knowledgeable and committed Jew, having been raised in an Orthodox home and later serving as both a religious school teacher and a superintendent. She was also a gifted preacher with well-developed skills as a conflict mediator and pastoral counselor–in short, a perfect candidate, one might think, for the Reform rabbinate. Perhaps Isaac Mayer Wise thought so too, although no written record of such thoughts survive.

What have survived, however, are newspaper reports from 1892 that announce the intention of the then thirty-one-year-old Ray Frank to "depart for the East to enter the Hebrew Union College as a theological student."[9] Also surviving are clippings from 1893, including one from Wise's own paper, the *American Israelite*, referring to Frank's "avowed purpose of entering the Jewish ministry." While the fact that Frank engaged a manager/lecture agent has led some to claim that she was motivated to enroll at HUC for reasons of self-promotion,[10] I find no convincing evidence that supports this assertion. Indeed, though Frank herself later wrote that she never had any intention of becoming a rabbi, her personal correspondence and actions, as recorded by newspapers both here and abroad, suggest that her abrupt departure from the College after less than a year of study was not part of her original plan.

Ray Frank is not alone in meriting our attention as one of a number of late-nineteenth- and early-twentieth-century women who might have become rabbis had the men in whose hands the privilege of ordination rested been willing to grant ordination to them. Isaac Mayer Wise admitted that one of the College's early female students "heartily wished to prepare herself for the pulpit." Yet we discouraged her, he said, "because it appeared to us [that] she had not the requisite oratorical capacity and without that success in the pulpit is not very likely."[11] So, apparently, did they discourage Lena Aronsohn, from Little Rock, Arkansas, who entered HUC at the same time as Ray Frank with the expressed desire of becoming a rabbi.[12] No less discouraged within the Conservative movement was Henrietta Szold. Despite her own insistence that she had no ambition to become a rabbi, she would have been an immensely qualified applicant for the Jewish Theological Seminary's rabbinic program. Indeed, she took courses at the seminary and in all likelihood *would* have sought ordination had she not been a woman.

In England it was not until 1956 (with the opening of the Leo Baeck College) that the Liberal Jewish movement began to train rabbis; and not until the mid-1960s did Leo Baeck College accept women as rabbinic students. Had the College opened in the 1920s or 1930s when joint sponsorship with Britain's more religiously conservative Reform movement was less likely to have occurred, Lily Montagu—founder of the Liberal Jewish movement and, by 1928, spiritual leader of the West Central Liberal Jewish Congregation—might well have become the first woman in Jewish history to be ordained as a rabbi.[13]

Instead, that honor rests with Regina Jonas, privately ordained in December 1935 by Rabbi Max Dienemann of Offenbach; Dienemann was a German Reform rabbi who was among the founders of the World Union for Progressive Judaism.[14] Though Jonas had previously completed her master's work in Jewish studies at the Hochschule für die Wissenschaft des Judentums (the Berlin Academy for the Scientific Study of Judaism), the Talmud professor empowered with ordaining her refused to do so on the grounds that she was a woman. In light of the fact that she had completed all of the requirements for ordination except the oral examinations that had been denied her, Dienemann took the unusual step of examining Jonas himself and, apparently satisfied with the results, privately granted her a Hebrew rabbinic diploma. While Jonas was sent letters of congratulations from various rabbinic and lay leaders of the German Jewish community, including Leo Baeck (who had previously signed a certificate testifying to her preaching abilities), she received no offers to serve as a congregational rabbi. She did, however, sign a contract with the Berlin Gemeinde (the Jewish community) to serve as both a religion teacher and a chaplain, visiting hospitals and senior citizen homes.[15]

By the end of the 1930s, as congregations increasingly lost their rabbis due to emigration, arrests, deportations, and deaths, Jonas found that she was increasingly called upon to preach. She worked in Berlin until 1942, when she was deported to Terézin. Katharina von Kellenbach, who has done extensive work on Jonas, has discovered a list of lectures as well as a sermon that she delivered there.[16] Approximately two years later, Regina Jonas died in Auschwitz.

In the United States, the issue of women's ordination was first formally considered by the faculty of HUC, its board of governors, and members of the CCAR as a whole during a two-year period spanning from 1921 through 1923. In late spring 1921, seventeen-year-old Martha Neumark, a student at the College since 1919 and daughter of David

Neumark, professor of Jewish philosophy at HUC, petitioned the faculty to be assigned to lead High Holy Day services in the fall, should a pulpit become available. The faculty's vote ended in a tie, and it was left to Kaufmann Kohler, then president of the College, to resolve the matter. Kohler voted to approve Neumark's petition subject to subsequent approval by the congregation in question. He also resolved to form a joint faculty/board of governors committee to consider the larger issue that the petition had indirectly raised—namely, given the Reform movement's commitment to women's religious equality, why should qualified women not be granted rabbinic ordination?

The report adopted by the joint committee maintained that its members saw "no logical reason why women should not be entitled to receive a rabbinic degree." It went on, however, to state: "Because of practical considerations, your committee is of the opinion that the admission of women to the Hebrew Union College with the aim of becoming rabbis, should not be encouraged."[17] The board of governors received copies of the majority report and a dissenting report submitted by two of the six committee members: Oscar Berman, a member of the board, and Jacob Lauterbach, professor of Talmud. Included among the objections to women's ordination that Berman and Lauterbach presented were: the opposition expressed in Jewish tradition and religious teachings; the fact that to most Jews "such an innovation would seem absurd and ridiculous"; the belief that the ordination of women would be a "bad investment" because once a woman rabbi married "she would very likely leave the rabbinate"; and the fear that female students would distract "some of the [male] students from their work."[18]

Unable to reach a decision, the board of governors referred the issue to the HUC faculty, asking for their opinion as to whether halakhah in fact prohibited the ordination of women as rabbis. After a great deal of debate and despite his continuing, personal opposition, Lauterbach reluctantly proposed that "in view of the fact that Reform Judaism has in many other instances departed from traditional practice, it cannot logically and consistently refuse the ordination of women."[19] The faculty subsequently voted unanimously to approve his resolution. The board then referred the matter to the CCAR. By a vote of 56-11, it too affirmed that women could not "justly be denied the privilege of ordination."[20] Rather than arguing, in other words, *for* women's ordination (perhaps based on Reform's understanding of progressive revelation or on the need to create a Judaism more in keeping with the spirit of the modern age), supporters of the CCAR resolution simply maintained that *given* all that Reform stood for (or did not stand for, including strict observance of traditional Jewish practice), there were no legitimate reasons for denying women the opportunity to become Reform rabbis. Given this lackluster endorsement, it is not surprising that a year later the board of governors overturned the CCAR recommendation. In justifying their actions, members of the board said that they did so not because they disagreed with the CCAR but simply because they felt that practical considerations outweighed philosophical ones. Given the social climate—that is, that women as religious leaders in Protestant America were the exception rather than the rule and that Jewish women as a whole were not clamoring for entrance into the rabbinate—there seemed to be no reason, they said, to "change the present practice of limiting to males the right to matriculate for the purpose of entering the rabbinate."[21]

In 1956 a CCAR committee was formed by Barnett Brickner, then president of the Conference and a strong advocate of women's ordination, to reconsider the issue. Perhaps members of the CCAR felt that the social climate had changed sufficiently to reopen the issue of women's ordination. Indeed, as Brickner himself pointed out, a significant number of mainline Protestant denominations in the United States had already begun to admit women into their seminaries and to ordain them as ministers, while a number of women had sought ordination throughout the history of HUC and Stephen Wise's Jewish Institute of Religion, which merged in 1950. Among them, I might add, was Helen Hadassah Levinthal, who claimed that by 1939 she had completed the entire rabbinic course at JIR.[22]

By 1956, two women, at least, despite their lack of rabbinic training, had in fact already succeeded in becoming Jewish religious leaders. The first, Tehilla Lichtenstein, assumed spiritual leadership in 1938 of the New

York-based society of Jewish Science, a Jewish countermovement to Christian Science. While Jewish Science did not formally affiliate with Reform,
its major proponents (with the exception of Tehilla Lichtenstein but including her husband, Morris Lichtenstein, the society's founder) were
Reform rabbis, all of whom were members of the CCAR and some of
whom attempted throughout the 1920s and 1930s, with little success, to
get the CCAR to formally approve its understanding of spiritual healing as
central to Jewish religious life. Thus, in 1956 members of the Conference
were not unaware of Tehilla Lichtenstein's achievements. Indeed, by 1956
she had been leader of the society for almost twenty years—a position that
she retained until her death in 1973.

Perhaps more influential was Paula Ackerman who in 1951, following
the death of her husband, William Ackerman, assumed spiritual leadership
of the congregation that he had led in Meridian, Mississippi. Ackerman
continued to serve as "lay rabbi" of Temple Beth Israel through the fall of
1953. During her tenure, she regularly led services, preached, and conducted weddings, funerals, and even conversions. According to Ackerman,
members of the Reform rabbinate whom she knew encouraged her in her
work and treated her with great respect.[23] Correspondence between Maurice
Eisendrath, then president of the Union of American Hebrew Congregations (UAHC), and Sidney Kay, president of the temple, indicates that
initially Eisendrath gave his approval to the congregation's request that
Ackerman become their leader. His reasons for doing so may well have
stemmed from the desire by at least some Reform rabbis, Eisendrath included, to see whether women could gain congregational acceptance as
religious leaders, thus paving the way for the entrance of women into the
Reform rabbinate itself.[24]

This theory concerning rabbinic interest in Ackerman's tenure at
Temple Beth Israel is strengthened by Michael Meyer's claim that by the
end of the 1940s "Hebrew Union College found itself hard pressed to
keep up with the demand for rabbis." Responding as best it could to
Reform's increased congregational growth, mirroring congregational growth
in the United States in general, HUC introduced a more active recruit-
ment program and in 1950 merged with the Jewish Institute of Religion.

Consequently, Meyer writes, "from less than 500 rabbis in 1943, [CCAR] membership rose to 850 in 1964 and grew even more rapidly thereafter."[25]

Finally, a new receptiveness to the idea of women as rabbis in 1956 may be attributed to a change in leadership. Certainly, the membership of the HUC Board of Governors had changed since 1922 as had the presidency of the College and its power in relationship to the board. Indeed, even before the CCAR committee voted to support the entrance of women into the rabbinate, HUC president Nelson Glueck publicly expressed his endorsement of the proposed resolution and stated that HUC-JIR would ordain any woman who passed the required courses.[26]

Despite this endorsement, however, the CCAR voted to table action on the committee's recommendation that women be ordained so that "those who have an opposite point of view may have an opportunity to present a report." Yet as Jane Evans, executive director of the National Federation of Temple Sisterhoods (NFTS), pointed out seven years later, no such report was ever offered and no action was taken either by HUC-JIR or by the CCAR. In marking the fiftieth anniversary of NFTS (which, even under the leadership of its founding president, Carrie Simon, had supported women's equality in Jewish life), members of the sisterhood voted to adopt a resolution calling for a conference of representative leaders of the CCAR, UAHC, HUC-JIR, and NFTS to determine what appropriate action should be taken concerning the matter of women's ordination.[27]

Such a conference never took place. Nor, apparently, did the 1963 sisterhood resolution elicit any formal response from HUC-JIR, the CCAR, or the UAHC. Indeed, women's journey to ordination reached its successful conclusion neither in the midst of any major controversy nor in a ground swell of movement-wide support. In the late 1960s, a young woman named Sally Priesand, after receiving a joint bachelor of arts degree from HUC-JIR and the University of Cincinnati, decided to continue her studies at HUC-JIR. "My decision to enter HUC's rabbinical program came about with little fanfare," she said later.[28] Apparently she, like many of the men who graduated with her, simply entered the program without undergoing either a formal interview or application process. That Priesand completed her rabbinical studies and received ordination testifies, I think, both to her tenacity and to the support of members of the faculty and administration, most notably Nelson Glueck and his successor in 1971, Alfred Gottschalk.

Some twenty years after Sally Priesand's ordination, we have much to celebrate. As of June 1993, 205 women will have been ordained as Reform rabbis, including Naamah Kelman, whose historic ordination in Israel took place in 1992.[§] By June 1994, 50 women will have been ordained from the Jewish Theological Seminary, 52 from the Reconstructionist Rabbinical College, and 16 from Leo Baeck College.[29] I am old enough to remember the time when I could honestly say that I knew, or knew of, every woman who had been ordained as a rabbi. It is a measure of how far we, as Jewish women, have come that today such a statement is an impossible one for me and, I suspect, for anyone to make. Yet if we use the same measure to reflect upon the number of women who are senior rabbis of large congregations, leaders of the CCAR, the UAHC, the Rabbinical Assembly, the United Synagogue, or faculty members of our rabbinical seminaries, we realize how far we still have to go. The truth is many of us can *still* claim to know or know of every woman who occupies such a position.

So, yes, let us celebrate, because there is much cause for celebration. But at the same time, as we look back upon women's journey towards rabbinic ordination, let us remember that in the end women achieved ordination because the men in whose hands the power of ordination rested finally decided to ordain them. It was not a question of women not being interested in the rabbinate until the late 1960s; as I have tried to show, women's interest in the rabbinate has been long-standing. The eighty-year gap between Ray Frank's short-lived tenure as a theological student at HUC and Sally Priesand's ordination should caution us against complacency, against sitting back and thinking: "If I only wait a little while, I know things will change." As we look toward the future, we might bear in mind, then,

---

[§] As of June 1995, 239 women have been ordained by HUC-JIR.

that perhaps one of the many lessons of women's journey toward ordination is that none of us can afford to invest in others our own hopes for
change.

Notes

1. David Philipson, *The Reform Movement in Judaism* (New York: Ktav, 1967), 140, 219, 220.

2. Ibid., 219.

3. Isaac Mayer Wise, *Minhag America: The Daily Prayers for American Israelites* (1857; reprint, Cincinnati: Bloch and Co., 1872) 12, in the section introducing the morning prayers. I am grateful to David Ellenson for bringing this reference to my attention.

4. Kaufmann Kohler, "Conference Paper," in "Authentic Report of the Proceedings of the Rabbinical Conference Held at Pittsurgh, Nov. 16, 17, 18, 1885," reprinted in Walter Jacob, ed., *The Changing World of Reform Judaism: The Pittsburgh Platform in Retrospect* (Pittsburgh: Rodef Shalom Congregation, 1985) 96. The Pittsburgh conference is historic because out of it emerged the Pittsburgh Platform, a statement of the principles on which Classical Reform Judaism in the United States rested.

5. Riv-Ellen Prell, "The Vision of Woman in Classical Reform Judaism," *Journal of the American Academy of Religion* 50, no. 4 (December 1982): 576.

6. Jacob Rader Marcus, "An Eleven Year Old Girl in 1875 Paved the Way for Women Studying for the Rabbinate Today," Philadelphia *Jewish Exponent*, 1972, copy in "Women Rabbis," Miscellaneous File, American Jewish Archives, Cincinnati.

7. Michael A. Meyer, *Hebrew Union College-Jewish Institute of Religion at One Hundred Years*, (Cincinnati: Hebrew Union College Press, 1976), 18.

8. Ibid., 36.

9. Ray Frank Litman papers, American Jewish Historical Society, Waltham, Mass.

10. Reva Clar and William M. Kramer, "The Girl Rabbi of the Golden West," pt. 3, *Western States Jewish History* 18 (1986): 345 ff. I am grateful to Jonathan Sarna for bringing this three-part essay to my attention.

11. Cited in ibid., pt. 1, 108.

12. Ibid., 109-110, citing the *Jewish Progress*, May 26, 1893. I have been unable to locate any surviving records that would indicate whether Aronsohn and the other female rabbinic aspirant about whom Wise spoke were the two women to have received a bachelor of Hebrew literature degree by 1900.

13. Though Lily Montagu herself might not have sought entrance into rabbinical school, she might well have been encouraged to do so by Israel Mattuck, rabbi of the Liberal Jewish Synagogue, who encouraged her as early as 1918 to preach from the *bimah*, and later encouraged her (as did Claude Montefiore, president of the Liberal Jewish movement and of the World Union for Progressive Judaism, conceived of by Lily Montagu in 1926) to assume a position of religious leadership. In 1944 the rabbinic leadership of the movement formally inducted Lily Montagu as a "lay minister."

14. Rabbi Dienemann was also a supporter and friend of Lily Montagu.

15. Her official title was "Seelsorgerin," a spiritual adviser or clergyman.

16. Katharina von Kellenbach, "'God Does Not Oppress Any Human Being': The Life and Thought of Rabbi Regina Jonas," *Leo Baeck Institute Year-book* 39 (1994). I am extremely grateful to Katharina von Kellenbach for all of the information she has provided me about Jonas, both in her letter to me (dated October 9, 1992) and in a phone conversation held on January 27, 1993.

17. "Majority Report of the Committee on the Question of Graduating Women as Rabbis," HUC Correspondence, Miscellaneous File, American Jewish Archives.

18. "Minority Report of the Committee on the Question of Graduating Women as Rabbis," HUC Correspondence, American Jewish Archives.

19. Cited in Meyer, *At One Hundred Years*, 99.

20. *Central Conference of American Rabbis Yearbook* 22 (1922), 51.

21. Meyer, *At One Hundred Years*, 99.

22. The JIR faculty seriously debated the issue of Levinthal's ordination but decided that the time was not yet right to ordain a woman as rabbi. As a compromise, she was given as master of Hebrew literature degree and a certificate in Hebrew designating that she had completed the curriculum. (Rabbi Israel Levinthal to Professor Jacob Marcus, April 14, 1972, Correspondence File, American Jewish Archives.) Whether she in fact completed the rabbinic program at JIR remains in dispute.

23. This description of her treatment was repeated to me by Paula Ackerman on numerous occasions from 1984 to 1989 at her homes in Atlanta and Thomaston, Georgia.

24. In one letter, dated December 1950, for example, Maurice Eisendrath wrote to Sidney Kay: "I will be especially interested in learning whether Mrs. Ackerman does accept [the congregation's offer] and will appreciate being kept informed as to the reaction in your congregation and community...I wish to emphasize my genuine desire to hear from you as I may possibly make some comment on this step that you have taken in some future reference either by the spoken or written word." Ackerman File, American Jewish Archives.

25. Michael A. Meyer, *Response to Modernity: A History of the Reform Movement in Judaism* (New York: Oxford University Press, 1988), 359.

26. *New York Times*, November 21, 1963.

27. Resolution on Ordination of Women as Rabbis, Adopted by 24th Biennial Assembly of NFTS. My thanks to Jane Evans for supplying me with a copy of this resolution.

28. Conversation with Rabbi Sally Priesand, Monmouth Reform Temple, Monmouth, N.J., February 1, 1991.

29. I am grateful to Dr. Gary P. Zola, National Dean of Admissions at HUC-JIR, for supplying me with these figures.

From Antoinette Brown Blackwell to Sally Priesand:

An Historical Perspective on the Emergence of Women in the American Rabbinate

Jonathan D. Sarna

In planning to speak at this conference, the question naturally arose as to how Ellen Umansky and I should divide the subject of the historical background to the emergence of women in the American rabbinate. Ellen and I spoke, and we decided on what seemed like a fair 50-50 division: she took on the Jewish aspects of the story, and I agreed to cover everything else.

My story begins early in the nineteenth century during the period known to American religious historians as the Second Great Awakening. In some respects, this was an era similar to our own: a time of remarkable religious change, with thousands of individuals undergoing religious revival (today we would say that they were "born again"), and a time when American religion itself was being transformed with the growth of new religious movements (some of which started as obscure sects and cults) and the acceptance of a host of new ideas. The most important of these ideas, for our purposes, was a diminished belief in predestination and innate human depravity and a greater emphasis on the ability of human beings, through their own efforts, to change and improve the world.

The transforming effects of the Second Great Awakening had a particular impact on women. Already in colonial times, American women had been deeply involved in religious life as church members, but now for the first time they found themselves enabled, even encouraged, to move beyond passive membership to take an active role in the great task of improving the world so as to speed the onset of the millennium. As historically powerless groups usually do when offered a new opportunity, they seized it and ran with it. "Women's prayer groups, charitable institutions, missionary and education societies, Sabbath School organizations and moral reform and maternal associations all multiplied phenomenally after 1800," a phenomenon that historian Nancy F. Cott has amply documented.[1] Through these organizations, often for the first time in their lives, women spoke out publicly and came to exercise spiritual and political leadership beyond the confines of their homes. These organizations served as a kind of lay ministry for some women, and they paved the way for more.

Let me point out in passing that a number of American Jewish women were influenced by some of these same currents. In concert with her Christian colleagues, for example, Rebecca Gratz of Philadelphia in 1801 helped to organize the Female Association for the Relief of Women and Children in Reduced Circumstances as well as fuel and sewing societies. She later worked to establish similar organizations for Jewish women: the Female Hebrew Benevolent Society and most important of all, the Hebrew Sunday School Society, which offered middle and upper class Jewish women some of the same kinds of opportunities for spiritual service—what we might today call religious action—as their Protestant sisters enjoyed. In a similar vein, the liturgical creativity of Penina Moïse in pre-Civil War Charleston reflects the religious awakening of women in this era. Prior to the nineteenth century we know of very few hymns by women, Christian or Jewish; beginning in this period we find them in growing numbers.[2]

"As opportunities for women in lay ministries proliferated," Ruth A. Tucker and Walter Liefeld write in their book, *Daughters of the Church*, "the door slowly opened for women to become involved in professional ministry. At first the only 'approved' ministries were ones that were strictly in the women's sphere—such activities as social work and writing—but even-

tually more and more women ventured into the male domain of evange-
lism and preaching."[3]

The word "eventually," even in this American Protestant context, carries a wide range of meanings. We know that among Baptists and Methodists, especially on the frontier, a few exceptional women—usually, by the
way, single women—"heard the call" and took up preaching, albeit without
the benefit of ordination and without having their own parish. It is said of
one Mary Savage, who preached in New England as early as 1791, that "the
smelting power of her exhortations was often irresistible." Clarissa Danforth,
in the second decade of the nineteenth century, was described (with considerable exaggeration) as "the sensation preacher of the decade."[4] None
of these women, however, occupied mainline churches. Indeed, in Protestantism as also in Judaism, women enjoyed far greater opportunities outside of the mainstream (whether they were geographically remote or religiously remote) than they did at the center.

This point brings me to a remarkable person who is rarely discussed
when we consider the roots of women in the American rabbinate and upon
whom I therefore want to focus. She is the "Sally Priesand" of American
Protestantism, the first woman of any denomination to be ordained in
America: the Reverend Antoinette Louisa Brown (later Brown Blackwell).

She was born in 1825 in what was then a great center of American
religious ferment, western New York, in the village of Henrietta. Like so
many others at that time, her father was deeply affected by the revivalistic
preaching of Charles Grandison Finney, and he returned to religion, bringing
his whole family with him. Religion and education played an important
role in Antoinette Brown's upbringing. Because she was bright and apparently had no aptitude whatsoever for domestic chores, which she hated,
she was permitted to attend a secondary school, the only one in the county
and therefore open to men and women alike. She graduated in 1840 at the
age of fifteen and was immediately invited to assume a job as a teacher of
young children.

"At some point during her teens," her biographer Elizabeth Cazden
reports, "Antoinette formulated the ambition that would thrust her into
historical prominence: She wanted to become a minister. It was not un-

usual for young women to show a strong interest in religious work during the 1840s. The world around them was changing rapidly...Many people felt confused about what part they should play in the new order. This identity crisis particularly affected young single women, and frequently made them open to greater involvement in religious activities. Despite other changes in their lives, they could still play an important part in society through the church and the various social reform organizations. In fact, both women and the church would increasingly be called upon to preserve and represent values of cooperation, sharing and nurturing that were cast aside by the prophets of economic progress. Women were not, however, expected to become public leaders of the religious community."[5]

Undaunted, Antoinette Brown took off for Oberlin College, presided over by the same Charles Finney who had so influenced her father years before. It was then a new college, sponsored by the Congregationalist Church, and it had a well-deserved reputation for radicalism, both because of its staunch abolitionism and because it opened its doors to women. (The first women recipients of baccalaureate degrees in the United States are all Oberlin graduates.) In four years she completed the literary course, received special limited permission to study theology, and published an article on the position of women in the New Testament. But in the end, Oberlin refused to ordain her. "They were on the very brink of the fatal spring over the great wall of custom," Brown wrote in a letter to her good friend Lucy Stone, later her sister-in-law and a well-known feminist and suffragist. "A little more and I should have been a man acknowledged minister, but somebody happened to think that though a woman might preach she ought not to administer the sacraments, &c. Others thought this and that, so they joined hands and turning round walked backwards together, and I took up my bundle and walked home."[6]

Fortunately for Brown (and for us), she was hired by a tiny Congregationalist church in South Butler, New York. The church turned to her, apparently, because nobody else would accept the paltry $300 annual salary that the parish could afford. So it was, from the beginning, that women were condemned to the lower-status and lower-paying jobs in the profession. For a time, nevertheless, she was satisfied. "The pastoral labors at S.

Butler suit me even better than I expected," she wrote, "and my heart is full of hope."[7] Within a few months, the church decided formally to ordain its new woman pastor—a step that was fully in keeping with Congregation-alist policy (many Congregationalist ministers were ordained by their churches rather than by their seminaries). There was some trouble locating a minister to perform the ordination, but finally a nearby Methodist minister agreed to do the honors, aided by the abolitionist reformer Gerrit Smith. Thus, on September 15, 1853, surrounded by a large crowd of friends and neighbors and in the midst (inevitably) of a violent rainstorm, Antoinette Brown was ordained. Two months later, she officiated at her first wedding—an event widely noted in the American press as the first American marriage ever solemnized by a woman. One month after that she delivered a lecture that won her the following accolade. (Remember that public speaking was a critical, almost a threshold skill that women who sought to achieve public status at that time needed to acquire).

> Her lecture was sprinkled all over with rich metaphors, with graphic figures, and that rare quality of modern productions, originality. The ideas expressed were clothed in beautiful language, such as none but the finest intellectual gifts could produce, sentences superbly framed, periods rounded with a grace not surpassed by the numberless gems of the great English essayists...There is not one that did not leave the hall with the most profound respect for the rare mental endowments of the speaker.[8]

This outward success, however, masked inner problems. As a result, only eight months later, in July 1854, Antoinette Brown resigned from her parish in South Butler. Loneliness, depression, a crisis of faith, tensions within her parish (especially with women church members), personal and professional insecurity, a sense that her feminist friends such as Susan B. Anthony, Elizabeth Cady Stanton, and Lucy Stone had turned away from her now that she had cast her lot with organized religion—all of these factors compounded by a breakdown in her physical health led Brown to return to the protective womb of her parental home to rest. She would never formally minister to a church again.

Instead, once she recovered, she turned to the other vehicle through which women of her day could affect her world: She took up writing, encouraged by Horace Greeley of the *New York Tribune*. Two years later, in 1856 (at the age of thirty-one), she married a businessman from Cincinnati named Samuel Blackwell. We would consider him a "liberated man," given the encouragement that he gave to his wife's activities and more substantively, his willingness to take upon himself the domestic chores that she so disliked. (He even came from a liberated family: His brother married Lucy Stone; his sister, Elizabeth, became one of the nation's first woman doctors.) Together the couple had seven children, five of whom lived beyond infancy. The Reverend Antoinette Brown Blackwell, as she now called herself, remained–although not without considerable difficulty–actively involved in the women's movement, delivering lectures around the country, promoting women's rights and suffrage, establishing credentials in science (we would say social science), writing eight books and countless articles, helping to found the Association for the Advancement of Women, and maintaining her lifelong interest in religion and theology. She may not have held her own parish, but she ministered to her friends. "Everybody leaned on her," one acquaintance recalled. "Hers was the true vocation of the clergyman."[9] In her late seventies, having become a Unitarian, Brown Blackwell helped to establish a Unitarian society in her new hometown of Elizabeth, New Jersey. In recognition of her services, she was appointed "minister emeritus" and she took up her old skills, preaching there once a month until she turned ninety. At age ninety-five, she voted in her first presidential election, having lived long enough to see the women's suffrage amendment enacted. A year later, she died peacefully in her sleep.

The story of Antoinette Brown Blackwell's career seemed to me worth recalling here for two reasons. First, her pioneering experiences as America's first woman clergyperson suggests certain themes that have continuing relevance. The travails that she experienced both in her studies and in her first position, her inner religious doubts, her later conflict between the demands of family and the demands of public life, and her decision not to pursue a minister's standard career path–all these were themes that would continue to characterize the experiences of women clergy down to our own day. As we consider some of these same themes at this conference it is, I think, well to recall that women have been grappling with these issues for a long time, even before 1972.

It is no less significant to point out that in her own way, using the knowledge, the skills, the professional competence, and even the title that she acquired in becoming a minister, Brown Blackwell did ultimately help to change the world: through her writings, through her lectures, through her work on behalf of women's rights. Ministerial training for her was a form of what would today be called "radical empowerment": It liberated her from the shackles that held back most mid-nineteenth-century women, and it gave her the confidence to tackle some of the great social and religious issues of her day. I would argue that women's ordination is still an act of radical empowerment. Historians who look back a century from now on today's women rabbis will, I think, again see, just as we do looking back at Antoinette Brown Blackwell, how significant professional training and the act of ordination have been in transforming lives: women rabbis' own lives (whether or not they choose the congregational rabbinate), the lives of those they touch, and ultimately the Jewish community and American society as a whole.

There is, however, a second observation about Antoinette Brown Blackwell's career that seems to me no less relevant. Her pioneering success was not followed by a great movement of other women into the clergy ranks.[10] The 1880 census listed some 165 women ministers with parish jobs, 33 of whom were Unitarians or Universalists. Other women rose to positions of leadership in some of the smaller religious movements, like the Spiritualist movement in the mid-nineteenth century, which granted women complete equality,[11] and later the Holiness movement, the Pentecostal movement, and Christian Science, where women played an important role from the beginning. Taken all together, however, we are talking about a very small number of women indeed. Most nineteenth-century Americans continued to think of religious leadership as a male preserve.

Protestantism offered women a far more significant public role in the realm of religious and social action. In the United States, Protestant women could serve as missionaries (foreign and domestic), as deaconesses, and as religious educators—all roles that opened up totally new opportunities for women in the nineteenth and early twentieth centuries. Protestant women were also encouraged to battle on behalf of great religious and social causes, the best known being temperance, a movement in which women played a particularly significant part. These various opportunities gave Protestant women greater visibility, as well as leadership experience, and a sense of religious self-worth. They prepared the groundwork, in many ways, for the ordination that came later.

Judaism, by contrast, was much slower to open up significant religious vocational opportunities to women. Admittedly, the Jewish Sunday school, Jewish women's benevolent societies, Jewish immigrant aid organizations, and especially Hadassah, the Zionist women's organization, did provide women with some of these opportunities. The early Hadassah nurses' settlements had much in common, functionally speaking, with Protestant women's foreign missions. Nevertheless, Jews were never historically as successful as Protestants in summoning women to work for social betterment within the context of their faith; certainly, Judaism never offered women a bona fide religious title on a par with missionary or deaconess. As a result, Jewish women have lacked the kinds of female religious role models that Protestants have had in comparative abundance; Henrietta Szold, I think, is the exception that proves the rule. This absence of exemplars probably made it more difficult for Jewish women to gain ordination and then to win acceptance from their congregants.

Still, even in American Protestantism, the ordination of women only began to become normative in mainline denominations in the 1950s. The Presbyterian Church (northern) and the Methodist Church both voted to ordain women in 1956, and at about the same time both Harvard and Yale Divinity Schools began to accept women into their programs on an equal basis with men. In 1970, two major Lutheran denominations voted to ordain women. In 1972, when Sally Priesand was ordained, fully 3,358 women were enrolled in major American theological seminaries, representing about 10 percent of students then studying for ordination.[12]

Thus, the decision to ordain women for the rabbinate, while a pathbreaking step for the Reform movement and for American Judaism generally, did not break any new ground at all in terms of American religion. In fact, the Reform movement was a comparative latecomer to the process, coming 119 years after Antoinette Brown Blackwell was ordained and many years after liberal churches had begun to ordain women—not just the Unitarians and the Universalists but even, as we have seen, the Presbyterians and the Methodists. This fact should serve as a humbling reminder that American Judaism is not always in the forefront of change, nor does it blindly imitate every innovation in American Christianity according to some supposed rule that "as go the Gentiles so go the Jews." Instead, there has always been a much more complex (and sometimes an exceedingly slow) process by which reforms have been evaluated, a process that involves a careful balancing of tradition and change, costs and benefits, religious ideas and social realities.

Taking this point a step further, it seems to me (heretical as it may sound here) that Judaism—yes, even Reform Judaism—has not historically been at the forefront of change in American religious life. On the contrary, as a minority faith, rooted in a system of law, blessed with a long religious tradition, and cursed with a long history of persecution, Judaism has quite understandably been reluctant to lead the way into uncharted religious territory. *Initiatives* for change—in this case the ordination of women, but the same was true for mixed seating—have generally come from without. Progressive Judaism has then moved, almost always more quickly than other branches of Judaism, to *respond* to new social and religious developments, challenging other branches of Judaism to respond in kind.

Notes

1. Nancy F. Cott, *The Bonds of Womanhood* (New Haven, Conn.: Yale University Press, 1977), 132.

2. On Christian hymnody, see Erik Routley, *A Panorama of Christian Hymnody* (Collegeville, Minn.: Liturgical Press, 1979), 115, as cited in Ruth A. Tucker and Walter Liefeld, *Daughters of the Church* (Grand Rapids, Mich.: Zondervan, 1987), 256.

3. Tucker and Liefeld, *Daughters of the Church*, 253.

4. Quotes are from ibid., 258-59.

5. Elizabeth Cazden, *Antoinette Brown Blackwell: A Biography* (Old Westbury, N.Y.: Feminist Press, 1983), 14-15. Most of what follows is drawn from this fine biography.

6. Brown to Stone, August 4, 1852, in Carol Lasser and Marlene Deahl Merrill, *Friends and Sisters: Letters Between Lucy Stone and Antoinette Brown Blackwell, 1846-93* (Urbana: University of Illinois Press, 1987), 120.

7. Quoted in Cazden, *Antoinette Brown Blackwell*, 75.

8. Quoted in ibid., 62.

9. Quoted in ibid., 227.

10. For what follows, see ibid.; Tucker and Liefeld, *Daughters of the Church*, 245-400; Virginia Lieson Brereton and Christa Ressmeyer Klein, "American Women in Ministry: A History of Protestant Beginning Points," in *Women in American Religion*, edited by Janet Wilson James (Philadelphia: University of Pennsylvania Press, 1980), 171-90; Rosemary Radford Ruether and Rosemary Skinner Keller, eds., *Women & Religion*

in America: A Documentary History, 3 vols. (New York: Harper and Row, 1986), 3:223-383.

11. Ann D. Braude, "Spirits Defend the Rights of Women: Spiritualism and Changing Sex Roles in Nineteenth-Century America," in *Women, Religion and Social Change*, edited by Yvonne Yazbeck Haddad and Ellison Banks Findly (Albany: State University of New York Press, 1985), 419-32.

12. Brereton and Klein, "American Women in Ministry," 186-90; Tucker and Liefeld, *Daughters of the Church*, 376-89; Constant H. Jacquet, Jr., ed., *Yearbook of American & Canadian Churches* 58 (1990): 282.

A Contemporary Perspective

A Male God:

Dilemmas for Men as well as Women

Howard Eilberg-Schwartz

Not many generations live through a transformation of consciousness. But we are one of them. The shift in thinking that was occasioned by the women's movement has opened up a completely new way of thinking, a way of thinking that continues to overturn some of the most basic and cherished assumptions about what it means to be human. For those of us who have been part of that transformation—and not all of our generation have been—nothing in the landscape remains quite the same.

We look at the same tradition as our predecessors, but we see something radically different. We have learned to see gender—the representation of men's and women's experiences—as a role that boys and girls learn on the way to adulthood. For much of history gender was assumed to be natural, brute fact, inscribed by God or biology in the very fabric of our bodies. The realization that gender is learned, that as babies we have not yet taken the steps to become the girls and boys or women and men that we will one day become, has enabled us to begin seeing how symbols embedded in the myths, stories, fairy tales we learned as children played a role in turning us into the women and men we have become.

This transformation has ineluctably changed how we think about Judaism and religion. We have learned that religion is one of the cultural systems, perhaps one of the most important of them, that helps to promote gender roles and images. In particular it is in conceptions of God

57

that images of gender find some of their strongest expressions. Before the 1970s the question of God's gender was not an issue. Because God had no body, it was thought that God also had no gender. Or to put it more accurately, God's masculinity was so taken for granted that it was invisible.

It is fair to say that the predominantly male or masculine image of the Jewish God has been one of the most pressing theological problems for Jewish feminists over the past twenty years. In the wake of Mary Daly's *Beyond God the Father*, Jewish feminists such as Rachel Adler, Judith Plaskow, Marsha Falk, Ellen Umansky, and Rita Gross, among many others, noted the damaging effects on women of an image of God that is shot through with masculinity.[1] Not only is this God routinely described in masculine pronouns and adjectives throughout the Hebrew Bible and rabbinic tradition, but the predominant roles ascribed to this deity are masculine: God is a father, man of way, king, and so forth. To be sure, there are some feminine images of God, such as mother or nurse, as Phyllis Trible and Virginia Mollenkott have pointed out.[2] But these feminine images are in the minority. A predominantly masculine imaging of God, as we have learned, legitimates male domination in the social order. In the words of Judith Plaskow, "When God is pictured as male in a community that understands 'man' to have been created in God's image, it only makes sense that maleness functions as the norm of Jewish humanity."[3] Or in the words of Virginia Mollenkott, "It should surprise nobody that women are not as good at being *man* as men are."[4] In many ways, the past twenty years have been devoted to making this problem evident and exploring potential solutions. There have been many liturgical responses to this theological problem, ranging from use of goddess imagery to gender-neutral language.[5]

But there is another theological problem, whose awareness has thus far only been on the periphery of consciousness and whose formation I believe is equally important if we wish to understand the ways in which gender roles are embedded in Jewish tradition. The question is this: What are the consequences of a male image of God for human masculinity?

It is not surprising that this question has yet to be brought into focus. The first gender challenges to Jewish theology have been formulated by women exploring the ways in which femininity is imagined and the ways in which Jewish theology supports female subordination. It is only natural to assume from that position that an image of a male God is unproblematic for men. But as gender criticism has begun to reshape how I see things, and as I have begun to think about Jewish images of masculinity, I am no longer so sure. It seems to me that the time is not only ripe but urgent for us to begin thinking about the Jewish construction of masculinity. This task would involve understanding how masculinity is an ideal that is created through Jewish images, myths, and stories about what it is to be a man. This line of inquiry is a natural extension of the kinds of questions we have already learned to ask, for femininity and masculinity are part of a larger symbol system, an understanding of which cannot take place piecemeal.

One of the central questions in this new labor must be to consider the effects of a male image of God on representations of masculinity. Thus far gender criticism has treated masculinity as one undifferentiated category. If we break this category apart and treat human and divine masculinity as separate symbols, we begin to see that a male God generates certain dilemmas and contradictions for men as well as women. I have written a book on this subject, and in what follows I share some of my own ideas about this issue.[6]

While the image of a male father-God clearly legitimates male domination, it also raises some significant problems for men because religious symbols do more than simply reflect the social order. They are also objects of emulation and desire. That is to say, they are ideals to which people aspire but often cannot achieve, and they are images that people love and admire. Given this view of religious symbols, we can begin to see how a male deity poses an enormous set of problems for human masculinity.

First, the deity is conceptualized as a nonsexual being, while human males are defined at least in part through their ability to procreate and reproduce the genealogy of Israel. As has been pointed out by many interpreters, the God of the Jews, unlike the gods of the Ancient Near East and elsewhere, does not have sexual intercourse or reproduce or father children, at least in the official literature that made its way into the Hebrew Bible. It is true that this God metaphorically gets married (Hos.1-2; Jer.

2:2) and has sexual intercourse with Israel (Ezek. 16:8), who is imagined collectively as a woman. But these notions of sexuality, reproduction, and fatherhood are disembodied. They are metaphors to describe God's loving relationship with Israel. Yet, having sexual relations and reproducing is central to what this tradition regards as masculinity. To be a man, one must procreate and reproduce the lineage of the fathers.[7] There is a tension, therefore, between being made in the image of a male God who has no sexuality and being expected as a male to carry out one's duties of procreating and reproducing the genealogy of Israel.[8]

Second, the deity is sometimes regarded as competition for human males, inasmuch as the human male's ability to reproduce is dependent upon the will or participation of the deity. To be sure, the husband contributes the seed. But the contribution of the seed alone does not guarantee pregnancy. In numerous instances, the pregnancy of a woman is a sign of God's favor. The human husband must stand idly by and wait until her womb is opened by God. Because it is God the father who determines whether or not a woman conceives, the human male is in danger of being rendered superfluous. In this sense, the virility of the human male is potentially put at risk by representations of divine masculinity.

Third, and perhaps most important, the idea of a masculine deity poses a threat to the basic heterosexual assumptions and practices that inform this religious culture. This threat arises because the divine-human relationship is sometimes couched in erotic and sexual metaphors (e.g., God, the husband, marrying or making love to Israel, the wife). Yet this heterosexual image of divine husband and human wife actually belies the nature of the relationship in question: Human males, not females, are believed to have the most intimate relationship with the deity. Individual males have the desire both to know and to be known by God. Thus there is potentially a homoerotic relationship at the heart of a religious culture that treats male-male sexual relationships as an abomination.

Marriage and sexuality are favorite metaphors for describing God's relationship with Israel. In Hosea, Jeremiah, and Ezekiel, God is the husband and Israel is the wife. In both Hosea and Ezekiel we encounter images that suggest that espousal and even intercourse are metaphors for the covenant. And we know that when Israel follows other gods it is metaphorically considered to be whoring (Hos. 4:12-14; Jer. 2:20, 3:9, 13:27; Ezek. 16:14-28, 23:1-31). Israel's relationship with God is a monogamous sexual relation; idolatry is adultery.

At one level this image obviously supports the male position in marriage relationships. The husband is to the wife as God is to Israel. But if we consider matters further, this image turns out to conceal an ambiguity. God's primary relationships in the Hebrew Bible are with men: the patriarchs, Moses, and so forth. The Israel who is collectively imagined as a woman is really men who are in a loving relationship with God. This relationship would not pose a problem if human masculinity were not so strongly associated with procreation and hence heterosexuality. Male homosexual relationships are considered an abomination in Leviticus (18:20, 20:13), and the story of Sodom and Gomorrah (Gen. 19) seems to condemn Canaanites by associating them with homosexual desire.[9] Thus there is a tension: On the one hand, to be a man one must father children and reproduce the lineage of the fathers. But to be a man of God involves loving, in ways that are imagined erotically, a male father God. I am not saying that the love of a male God necessarily means a man has or is displacing homoerotic desire. But I am suggesting that the ancient Jewish symbol system has a contradiction in it. It is positing two conflicting images of men.

What evidence is there to support this claim that male love of a male God poses a dilemma? Signs of evasion suggest the presence of the problem. The first signs of evasion revolve around the cloaking of God's body. Since Philo, the Jewish God has generally been thought to be incorporeal of disembodies. Generally it is thought that Jews came to believe in an abstract, disembodied God in a process similar to that of the Greeks. My own thinking about the male gendering of God has brought me to question this oft-repeated assertion. Indeed, if we look at biblical tradition, we find no explicit statement that God is disembodied or incorporeal. Rather we find that God's image cannot be represented in plastic art (Exod. 20:4-23, 34:17; Lev. 19:4; Deut. 5:8, 27:15) and that God's image usually cannot be seen. In a few instances various leaders see God and when they do, God has the appearance of a human form. In Exodus 24:9-11, Moses, Nadab, Abihu, and the elders of Israel ascend the mountain and see the God of Israel, although the narrator only describes the pavement of sapphire that is under the deity's feet. In Exodus 33:17-23, Moses asks to see God, but God says no one may see the divine face and live. So God puts a hand over Moses and then removes it to allow Moses to gaze on the divine back. It does not really matter, for the present purposes, whether Jews really believed God had a body; what is significant is that when they imagined visualizing God they conceived of the deity in a human form, but a human form that was veiled.

The veiling of the divine image, I suggest, may be related to the dilemma of homoeroticism. On the surface, this connection may sound implausible. But what we consider plausible is often based on that to which we have become accustomed. Consider two facts: In the God sightings, the gaze is averted from the mid-section of the divine body as if to veil that very part of the body that normally reveals a person's sex. Moses and the elders see what is under God's feet (Exod. 24), and Moses sees only God's back (Exod. 33). Although the other male gods of the Ancient Near East are often depicted with long flowing beards, we do not even know whether this God is imagined with a beard. It is as if the sex of this God poses a problem that has to be veiled.

Another myth lends support to this line of interpretation: the myth of Noah's drunkenness. After debarking the ark, Noah plants a vineyard, gets drunk, and lies naked in his tent. His son Ham, whose name incidentally means "hot," sees his father's nakedness and reports Noah's exposure to his brothers. Ham's son Canaan is condemned for this act, thereby associating the Canaanites once again with homoerotic desire. The virtuous sons, Shem and Japeth, put a cloak on their backs and, walking backward, cover their father. Here then is a story that insists that a son must not gaze at his father's nakedness. There is a striking similarity between the story and the myth of God turning his back on Moses. In this way, Moses is prevented from looking inappropriately at God.

Because God is imagined as a father figure, the similarities between these stories are important. God must be approached with the same kind of delicacy as a son approaches his human father. The most graphic description of God, of course, is Ezekiel's vision of God on the chariot (Ezek. 1:26-28). Ezekiel describes God from the loins up and the loins down as if his gaze is drawn irresistibly to the deity's midsection. It is as if Ezekiel dares to imagine what other visions kept under wraps. Not surprisingly, Ezekiel's vision of God becomes esoteric doctrine in rabbinic Judaism and cannot be taught in public (Mishnah Hagigah 2:1). There is no final proof that the interpretation I am offering is correct, but it has as much plausibility and explains as much of the evidence as any of its competitors.

If one solution to the problem of male homoerotic desire for God is to veil the divine body, then another solution is to feminize Israelite males. To preserve the heterosexual imagery, Israelite men have to be regarded as wives of God. We have already seen this image operating in the view of an Israel who is imagined collectively as a female. But it also operates in the stories about individual males. Consider Moses, who has the most intimate relationship with God and is the only prophet to speak to God "mouth to mouth" (Num. 12:8). When Moses comes down off the mountain, his face is changed (Exod. 34:29-35). Interpreters do not know precisely what the biblical Hebrew means here: Is his face abeam with light? Or is it perhaps disfigured?[10] In any case, Moses veils his face because the people are taken aback by his appearance. The ostensive purpose of the veil is to hide Moses' face. But symbols are often multivalent, and it is significant that the veil is normally an article of female clothing. Moses is the only man in the Hebrew Bible to be described as wearing a veil. I suggest that Moses has been partly feminized in his relationship with God.

The risk of feminization, of losing one's masculinity as one becomes a man of God, is also evident in the story of Jacob's struggle with the angel (Gen. 32:23-33). As with many biblical stories that do not seem to fit a spiritual image of monotheism, interpreters often regard this story as a survival of an older myth that Israel preserved.[11] But why would Israel have preserved this myth unless it said something powerful? One thing it may suggest is that a man must symbolically sacrifice his masculinity as he becomes a man of God. Jacob, you will recall, is finally becoming a man in his own right. He has been a puppet of Laban for fourteen years and is finally returning to Canaan to face his brother and claim his inheritance. Thus at the precise moment he is becoming a man, he is attacked by a divine being who injures him as dawn is breaking. The injury is described as occurring in "the hollow of his thigh." The thigh is often a euphemism for the genitals, and a convincing argument can be made that Jacob suffers injury to his manhood.[12] Taken alone this analysis is probably not convincing. But I believe this connection between genital injury, unmanning, and circumcision also operates in the story of Dinah's rape (Gen. 34) and the attack on Moses in Exodus (4:24-26). Circumcision is not simply a symbol of fertility, as I have argued elsewhere, but also a sacrifice of masculinity and hence a feminization of Israelite men as they become men of God.

Because men have to be taken in the female position with respect to God, human women pose a threat to the relationship between men and God. This is a new way of thinking about the misogynist tendencies of Jewish tradition. Typically, women's inferior status in Judaism is regarded as the result of women's perceived otherness from men and a male God. But when images of heterosexual relationships structure the understanding of gender and desire, then a woman is the natural complement of a male God, for a male God is imagined in images of what men are naturally thought to have. The story of the sons of God who come down and cohabit with the daughters of men (Gen. 6:1-4) illustrates this complementarity. There is no room for human men on a heterosexual model of desire. I suggest that women are particularly threatening to men because they threaten to intrude on the male-male relationship, which is unstable. Women have to be defined as impure so that men can step into the feminine position with respect to God.

One myth illustrates this dynamic at work. Before the revelation on Sinai, God instructs Moses as follows: "Go to the people and warn them to stay pure today and tomorrow. Let them wash their clothes. Let them be ready for the third day; for on the third day the Lord will come down in the sight of all the people, on Mount Sinai" (Exod. 19:10-13). Note what happens, however, when Moses carries out God's instruction. Moses "warned the people to stay pure, and they washed their clothes. And he said to the people, 'Be ready for the third day: do not go near a woman'" (Exod. 19:15). There is a significant discrepancy between God's instructions to Moses and Moses' charge to the people. It is Moses and not God who insists that men not go near women. Most interpreters ignore or minimize the significance of this discrepancy, even though when Eve alters God's instruction in the Garden of Eden interpreters frequently take this act as a sign of her psychological state.

It seems almost self-evident and natural to interpreters that women must be avoided before an impending encounter with the sacred. But Moses' elaboration of God's instruction leaves an important ambiguity. Does the narrator wish the reader or listener to assume that Moses interpreted God's words properly? Or are we to understand that Moses' words reflect his understanding of what it means to stay pure? It seems plausible to assume that the narrator on some level wishes the reader to view the command to avoid women as Moses' *interpretation* of God's word. After all, God's instruction seems addressed to the Israelite people as a whole, including women; Moses is obviously directing his comments to the men alone. It is as if the narrator is recognizing on some intuitive level that the notion of women's impurity originates with human men and not with God. And it originates at the very moment when God calls men to face him. It is through Moses that the narrator expresses male anxieties about the promise of a God sighting. To be a man of God is to be in the position of wife. "Do not go near a woman" addresses the problem. When God approaches, men avoid women and cease temporarily to act as husbands. In this way, men collectively prepare themselves to be a feminine Israel. And by linking femininity and impurity, the natural complementarity between women and God is broken.

One implication of this analysis is a new way of thinking about the tenacious desire of men to keep women out of the pulpit. Women threaten to intrude on this intimate and potentially homoerotic father-son or male-male relationship. Furthermore, it puts to rest any claims that women's ordination or participation is problematic because women introduce a sexual energy or element into a sacred realm where it does not belong. The sexual element is already there. Women rabbis may interrupt a male-male eroticism, but they certainly are not responsible for the introduction of that eroticism into the sacred arena.

Another implication of this analysis is that this way of thinking also may give men alternative ways of thinking about an image of a male God. I myself found it impossible to find strength or comfort in a male image of God after the feminist critique. How could I be complicitous in female subordination? My own spiritual and emotional journey as a man has involved seeking a more intimate relationship with a father who was, like most men of his generation, emotionally distant. As part of this healing, I have found a need for loving images of a male father figure. There is always a danger for women in the idea of men celebrating an image of a loving male God. I hope that the next stage of our theological reflection will be able to recognize the need men have for loving fathers. Somehow we have to find a way to balance that need against the dangers of divinizing masculinity.

This interpretation also puts homoerotic love at the center of the theological tradition in a way that was previously not evident. While the tradition may dance around this love and find that love partially problematic, its presence is real and important in making the tradition what it is. This discovery can perhaps provide a resource for gay Jews who are struggling to see their experiences legitimated in the tradition.

The various arguments I have made about the dilemmas posed for men by a male God will have to remain at this point tantalizing suggestions. In some ways the specifics of the arguments are beside the point. At issue, rather, is taking the further step of beginning the process of understanding Jewish masculinity. Before the feminist critique of Judaism, we pretended to read Judaism simply as people, as if tradition had the same implications for us irrespective of our gender. Then we learned that there is a differential impact of women. We assumed, mistakenly I think, that we had already understood what Judaism had to say about masculinity. But that is a story I think we have only just begun to be told.

Notes

1. Mary Daly, *Beyond God the Father* (Boston: Beacon Press, 1973). Rachel Adler, "'A Mother in Israel': Aspects of the Mother-Role in Jewish Myth," in *Beyond Androcentrism*, edited by Rita Gross (Missoula, Mont.: Scholars Press 1977). Judith Plaskow, "The Right Question is Theological," in *On Being a Jewish Feminist*, edited by Susannah Heschel (New York: Schocken, 1983) 223-33. Marsha Falk, "Toward a Feminist Jewish Reconstruction of Monotheism," *Tikkun* 4 (4) (July/August 1989). Ellen M. Umansky, "Creating Jewish Feminist Theology: Possibilities and Problems," *Anima* 10 (1984): 133-34. Rita Gross, "Steps toward Feminine Imagery of Deity in Jewish Theology," in Heschel, *On Being a Jewish Feminist*, 234-47.

2. See Phyllis Trible, *God and the Rhetoric of Sexuality* (Philadelphia: Fortress, 1983). Virginia Mollenkott, *The Divine Feminine* (New York: Crossroad, 1983).

3. Judith Plaskow, *Standing Again at Sinai* (San Francisco: Harper, 1990).

4. Mollenkott, *Divine Feminine*, 3.

5. Marsha Falk, "Notes on Composing New Blessings: Toward a Feminist-Jewish Reconstruction of Prayer," *Journal of Feminist Studies in Religion* 3 (1) (Spring 1987): 39-53.

6. There is now archaeological evidence that some Israelites were worshipping Asherah as a partner of Yahweh. For references to this discussion, see Howard Eilberg-Schwartz, *God's Phallus and Other Problems for Men and Monotheism* (Boston: Beacon Press, 1994), 106.

7. On centrality of reproduction to masculinity in Judaism, see Howard Eilberg-Schwartz, *The Savage in Judaism: An Anthropology of Israelite*

Religion and Ancient Judaism (Bloomington: Indiana University Press 1990) and "The Problem of the Body for the People of the Book" in *People of the Body: Jews and Judaism from an Embodied Perspective*, edited by Howard Eilberg-Schwartz (Albany: State University of New York Press, 1991).

8.   Eilberg-Schwartz, "Problem of the Body."

9.   Alternate interpretations of this story have minimized the element of homoerotic desire. See, for example, John Boswell, *Christianity, Social Tolerance and Homosexuality* (Chicago: University of Chicago Press, 1980). For a critique of this view, see, for example, Eilberg-Schwartz, *God's Phallus*, 94-95, and David Greenberg, *The Construction of Homosexuality* (Chicago: University of Chicago Press, 1988), 195-96.

10. See, most recently, William H. Propp, "The Skin of Moses' Face—Transfigured or Disfigured?" *Catholic Biblical Quarterly* 29 (1987): 375-86.

11. I have discussed this spiritualizing tendency of modern interpretation in *Savage in Judaism* and in *People of the Body*.

12. See S.H. Smith, "'Heel' and 'Thigh': The Concept of Sexuality in the Jacob/Esau Narratives," *Vetus Testamentum* 40 (4) (1990): 464-73.

From Equality to Transformation:
The Challenge of Women's Rabbinic Leadership
Laura Geller

Twenty years ago some people thought we had come to the end of a journey, that we had reached the promised land of equality for Jewish men and women. After all, a revolution had occurred in Jewish life. Women could be rabbis.[1]

Twenty years ago I was a rabbinic student at Hebrew Union College-Jewish Institute of Religion (HUC-JIR) in New York. I studied in the old building on West Sixty-eighth Street, which was around the corner from where Sally Priesand was serving as the first woman rabbi. I was the only woman in my class, one of only two women rabbinic students in the New York school. My classmates were supportive and friendly; generally my teachers—all of whom were men—were rooting for my success. Most of them believed that because there were women rabbis and women rabbinic students, we had already succeeded in reaching equality and equal opportunity.

Few of them understood the particular pressures and the unique challenges that I experienced in my years at the College. Only other women understood the pain of patriarchal texts, the confusion of finding myself absent in the stories that shape our tradition, the desperate need to reenvision a Judaism that includes the experience of all Jews. Only other women understood the pressure of being a pioneer, of wanting to be considered as capable as the men without being forced to give up my own sense of balance, of wanting a life where work is a blessing within the context of other blessings—family, commitments, friends.

While these were problems only women understood twenty years ago, there were hardly any other women with whom to share these feelings. I felt as though I were wandering in the wilderness, lonely for the dancing of Miriam and the women.

What a difference two decades make! As of June 1994, 221 women will have been ordained as Reform rabbis,[§] and women now make up almost half the student body at HUC-JIR. By June 1994, 52 women rabbis will have been ordained by the Reconstructionist Rabbinical College and 50 by the Jewish Theological Seminary. Our lives as women who are rabbis are full of blessings: work that challenges and stimulates us; colleagues, both women and men, to share our struggles and our successes; partners, children, friends, community. We have much to celebrate.

Women rabbis have changed the face of Judaism. At the simplest level, the change is obvious. As Rabbi Ellen Lewis wrote a few years ago: "When I first assumed my present pulpit, I tried to do everything just like my predecessor did. I had great respect for his work in the congregation and was not looking to be revolutionary. I just wanted to be the rabbi. What I found was that, even if I did the same things he did, when I did it it looked and sounded different." At her first bat mitzvah as a student rabbi, a thirteen-year-old girl looked up at Ellen as they practiced on the pulpit and asked, "At my bat mitzvah do you think we can wear matching dresses?"

Other similar stories abound. Rabbi Deborah Prinz tells the story of her first Shabbat on the pulpit of Central Synagogue. Rabbi Sheldon Zimmerman had for years been changing the language of the prayerbook to make it gender-neutral. Rabbi Prinz read the prayerbook the same way. But at the end of the service a congregant came up to Rabbi Zimmerman to complain: "See, you hire a woman and the first thing she does is change the prayerbook!"

[§] As of June 1995, 239 women have been ordained by HUC-JIR.

At the conclusion of my first High Holy Days services as the rabbi at the University of Southern California, two congregants rushed up to me. The first, a middle-aged woman, blurted out: "Rabbi, I can't tell you how different I feel about services because you are a woman. I found myself feeling that if you can be a rabbi maybe I can be a rabbi too. For the first time in my life I felt as if I could learn those prayers, I could study Torah, I could lead this service, I could do anything you could do. Knowing that made me feel much more involved in the service—much more involved with Judaism! Also the service made me think about God in a different way, I'm not sure why." The second congregant had something very similar to say but with a slightly different emphasis. He was a man in his late twenties. "Rabbi, I realized that if you could be a rabbi then certainly I could be a rabbi. Knowing that made the service somehow more accessible for me. I didn't need you to do it for me. I could do it, be involved with Jewish tradition, without depending on you."

In each of these anecdotes, and there are hundreds more, the theme is the same: People experience women rabbis differently from the way they experience male rabbis. And that difference changes everything—the way they experience prayer, their connection to the tradition, and even their image of divinity.

When women function as clergy, the traditional American division between clergy and layperson begins to break down. A woman who is an Episcopal priest told me that when she offers the Eucharist, people take it from her differently from the way they would take it from a male priest, even though she follows the identical ritual. People are used to being fed by women, and so the experience is more natural, less mysterious.

People do not attribute to women the power and prestige that they often attribute to men. Therefore when women become rabbis, or clergy of any kind, there is often less social distance between the congregant and the clergy. The lessening of social distance and the reduction of the attribution of power and status lead to the breakdown of hierarchy within a religious institution. "If you can be a rabbi, then certainly I can be a rabbi!" "Can we wear matching dresses?"

Women rabbis have had a profound impact on the way many Jews experience divinity. While most of the systematic work in the area of Jewish feminist theology has been done by women scholars who are not themselves rabbis, the very presence of women rabbis has forced many congregants to confront God in different ways. Some Jews make an unconscious transference between their rabbi and God. As long as their rabbi is male, they are not even aware that they associate him in some way with a male divinity. But when the rabbi is female, they cannot make that unconscious transference—so they begin to confront directly their images of God and perhaps even open themselves to ask "Who is the God I experience and how can I speak toward God in prayer?"

Here too, while much of the most creative work in prayer and liturgy is being written by feminists who are not themselves rabbis, it is often women rabbis who are on the front line when it comes to liturgy.

Rabbis are on the front line of ritual work as well. Congregants come to their rabbis for help in negotiating the transitions of their lives—the joys and the losses. Women rabbis have created ceremonies and rituals to meet the real-life experience of the Jews they serve, and many of these rituals are for women. Covenant ceremonies for daughters, b'not mitzvah, weddings, divorces, ceremonies of healing from loss, miscarriage, abortion, infertility, adult survivors of childhood incest, turning fifty or sixty, children leaving home—these are all actual transitions in the lives of Jews that have led women rabbis to create ritual.

Along with other feminists—scholars, educator, cantors, laypeople—women rabbis have been part of the transformation of Judaism. After twenty years, we have much to celebrate.

But we also have reason to be concerned. Those who believed that the ordination of women itself was enough to bring us to the promised land of an egalitarian Judaism were wrong. Even after twenty years, after more than 200 women have been ordained by the Reform movement, significant differences still exist between the careers of men and women rabbis.

These differences are of great concern to me—so I would like to try to understand them. I focus my remarks on the Reform movement because it is the movement I know best, but I suspect that similar observations could be made about the Reconstructionist and Conservative movements as well.

Of the 221 Reform women rabbis already ordained, none serves as the head of a thousand-member congregation. This fact is particularly troubling given that the traditional measure of success for rabbis in the Reform movement is the size of their congregations.

What explains the fact that women rabbis are not assuming positions that Reform Judaism has defined as powerful? This phenomenon has been addressed in two different ways. The first way, what I would call the "different voice" theory, is best illustrated by an article by Rabbi Janet Marder published in the summer 1991 issue of *Reform Judaism*. Rabbi Marder suggests that women have not assumed positions that are considered powerful because women are choosing a different path. She describes how some women see themselves as agents for change, consciously attempting to redefine rabbinic leadership. Through conversation with different women rabbis, Rabbi Marder argues that many women rabbis share a commitment to three fundamental values that are central to their rabbinate: balance, intimacy, and empowerment.

The value of balance was repeatedly mentioned to Rabbi Marder in her interviews with women colleagues. Over and over again, women challenged the conventional view that the rabbinate must be an all-consuming lifetime calling. In the past, male rabbis have often tended to take pride in how many hours they devote to their work. Rabbi Marder found that many women emphasized the ways they have made room in their life for other priorities and have been willing to limit the hours spent in work. Some have chosen to work part-time, or serve smaller synagogues, or serve in rabbinic positions that require fewer evening or weekend commitments; others have accepted a lower salary for lighter responsibilities.

Given the high priority these women place on balance, it is not surprising that some women seem to be choosing different career paths from the one the Reform movement holds out as the "success track." Rabbi Marder quotes Rabbi Arnold Sher, director of the Reform movement's Placement Commission: "I have no statistical way of proving it, but my gut feeling is that most men in A congregations (up to 120 members) aspire to move into larger ones. It's very clear that women in AB congregations (166-300 members) are not seeking larger pulpits." Some women are choosing smaller congregations, which not only grant the rabbi more con-trol over her time and her schedule but also provide the opportunity to form intimate relationships and create community.

Many women rabbis echo the words of Reconstructionist Rabbi Sandy Sasso: "Women come to the rabbinate with a different set of experiences...Women's center of focus is on people rather than principles...Women's version of reality is not a hierarchical model where one's goal is to move up, to be alone at the top, but rather a network model where the goal is to connect with others, to be together at the center."

The "different voice" theory is compelling because it seems to de-scribe the personal choices of many women rabbis I know. In each individual case it makes sense that a particular woman has chosen a particular "alter-native" career path. But viewed as an aggregate, as a class of rabbis, the difference between men's and women's careers is stunning—and depress-ing.

Are we freely choosing this voice? Or is the "different voice" argument a justification for keeping some of us out of positions that have been de-fined as powerful?

An alternative way to understand the discrepancy in the career paths of men and women is to argue that there remains discrimination against women in the rabbinate—a glass ceiling. This argument takes into account the ob-stacles to equality that women rabbis still face.

First, significant salary discrepancies exist between women and men. Rabbi Mark Winer has been monitoring salary data for the Central Con-ference of American Rabbis (CCAR) for the past fourteen years. His data show an alarming disparity in wages between men and women in the rab-binate, with the wage gap getting larger the further one is removed from entry-level positions. At the middle-size congregation (more than 300 fami-lies), for example, no woman is even close to the median salary. It is hard to understand this discrepancy in any other way than as evidence of en-demic discrimination in the compensation of women rabbis around the country. While the CCAR and the Union of American Hebrew Congrega-tions (UAHC) have gone on record as deploring this salary gap, to date little has been done to try to remedy the problem.

A second problem relates to the specific pressures on women rabbis who become mothers. In the early years after the first ordination of a woman, there was a great deal of talk among women rabbis about maternity leave. We were advised back then to handle each situation as individuals and to wait until we had a solid and sure relationship with our congregation or community before we raised the question. The advice from the leadership of the Reform movement in those old days was that, while no congregation would refuse their beloved rabbi her maternity leave, they might not hire the rabbi in the first place if maternity leave was part of the rabbi's negotiation for the position. Now, twenty years later, the Reform movement has taken a proactive stance. The most recent guidebook for rabbinic congregational relations includes a recommendation for two months of paid maternity leave plus accrued vacation. It is far from perfect, and often congregations ignore it, but it is the beginning of the Reform movement's attempt to address the reality that in our society child care is still viewed as primarily the problem of women.

The decision on the part of the CCAR and the UAHC to articulate the norms for how women must be treated concerning maternity leave could provide an important precedent for the Reform movement to take real leadership in other areas where women rabbis are concerned. But, at least until now, there does not seem to be an attempt to confront other areas of inequality.

Many women are qualified to be considered to be rabbis of 1,000 member congregations given their year of ordination. Thus far, the Reform movement has left them alone to decide whether or not to apply for these positions. Most do not apply.

Part of the problem may be a failure of imagination. Many women colleagues have difficulty imagining being a senior rabbi because they have no models of women senior rabbis. Some women acknowledge that their own experience as assistant rabbis, particularly the ways they were treated by their seniors, discouraged them from even considering applying for a senior position. Other women rabbis have stated that they believe women are hired more quickly than men as assistants because male senior rabbis believe that women are more docile and easier to manage. The perception that success as an assistant requires docility may make it hard for women who have succeeded as assistants to imagine themselves as the ones in charge.

Recently a very talented woman colleague who had been serving as an associate rabbi was invited by her congregation to apply for the position as senior when it became vacant. She turned down the invitation to apply, preferring instead to serve as interim senior rabbi until an appropriate successor could be found. Among her concerns was the sense that she would not be able to handle the senior rabbi's job. However, after the year as interim rabbi, she *was* able to imagine herself as the senior rabbi. But by then it was too late.

Perhaps the Reform movement should have intervened as it finally did on the issue of maternity leave, interrupting the "normal" course of events to encourage the woman to apply or even suggesting that the congregation wait for a year before beginning its search.

In order for this kind of affirmative action or differential treatment to be considered, the Reform movement must first view women rabbis as a class and acknowledge that the structures that presently exist favor men by definition. Synagogues and other Jewish institutions as they presently exist assume, for example, that the rabbi is not the primary caretaker of a pre-school child. Women who are mothers are—as a class—frustrated when they imagine themselves as rabbis of institutions that claim to be gender-neutral but in fact assume a male standard. Gender then becomes a question of power—with maleness the norm and femaleness the deviation.

These obstacles to equality are ultimately about power. A fourth critical issue—also about power—is the representation of women in the structure of our movements. After twenty years there are still very few women faculty at the Hebrew Union College-Jewish Institute of Religion. Just a few months ago the Cincinnati campus hired its second woman faculty member in the Rabbinical School. As of this writing, Los Angeles has one and New York none. Only one woman holds the rank of academic head, and women constitute only 10 to 15 percent of the board of governors. Only one regional director of the UAHC is a woman. The relative absence of women in the academic and professional branches of Reform Judaism supports the reality that the institutions favor men by definition.

Finally, women will remain powerless to crash through the glass ceiling until we are free to talk about the full reality of being a woman in the working world—and being a woman working as a leader in a Jewish institution or congregation. The fifth and perhaps the most difficult obstacle to women rabbis is the reality of sexual harassment and violations of sexual boundaries. Many women colleagues have stories that are shared only in private conversations with other women. Some experiences relate to inappropriate comments made to us during interviews about physical appearance, clothes, or even the size of one's breasts. Other experiences relate to women rabbis being threatened by inappropriate sexual advances by board members. Some women rabbis even have memories (some distant and some recent) of inappropriate advances made by faculty or administrators at the Hebrew Union College.

The 1992 and the 1993 conventions of the Pacific Association of Reform Rabbis included sessions on sexual harassment. This is a good beginning. But there is still pressure on women rabbis to join a conspiracy of silence about boundary violations that male colleagues commit with congregants or staff. Therefore it is particularly welcome that the *CCAR Journal* will publish Rachel Adler's important work about the complicated issues of power involved in violations of sexual boundaries between rabbis and congregants, thereby opening up a public conversation about our power as counselors and the devastation that occurs when sexual boundaries are violated.

For women rabbis to feel safe we must see the official agencies of all of our movements reacting strongly to condemn all these violations, between senior rabbi and assistant, between rabbis and congregants, between powerful congregant and woman rabbi, between professor or administrator and student. All of the movements of American Jewish life must mandate effective education and training of all rabbis, investigate complaints, and develop and monitor a disciplinary procedure. The old message that these movements just look the other way and even reward violators with better jobs is a threatening message to women rabbis and congregants.

So how ought we to understand the difference between the careers of men and women rabbis? Ought we, along with Carol Gilligan, explain the different choices women make in light of women's different experience, which propels them to seek connection rather than hierarchy?[2] Or ought we, along with Catherine MacKinnon, counter that because women lack power and do not participate in making the rules, we have no alternative but to seek other, less powerful, opportunities?[3] Are women rabbis' choices affirmatively challenging the rabbinic establishment's view that bigger is better, that moving up and moving on is the way to define success, or are women not being given a chance to play on the same field? Are these different choices attributable to a different women's choice or to women being excluded from the dominant conversation?

The past twenty years show evidence of both possibilities—of exclusion and of different choices. Perhaps both are true. Or perhaps (a third possibility) we cannot even talk of the possibilities of different choices until we even out the playing field and acknowledge that the structures themselves must be transformed to make room for women's participation.

The experience of the past two decades has made clear that the ordination of women was just the beginning of our journey. Just as it took our people forty years of wandering in the desert to reach a rich and fertile promised land, the journey toward the promised land of an egalitarian Judaism is far from over. The years of wandering have provided a glimpse into the future, the opportunity to revolutionize old ways of thinking and to begin to shift the paradigm from equality between men and women to the transformation of Judaism itself. We are clearly not there yet—but even as the struggle for equality continues, we can begin to see the questions raised by transformation.

The impact of women rabbis on Judaism begins with the revolutionary idea that women's experience ought to be acknowledged and valued. This idea poses fundamental challenges to rabbinic Judaism. It means that women are subjects as well as objects, that women are fully part of the story of our tradition. It means we must wrestle with our sacred texts to hear the voices of women just as we need to wrestle with the structures of our modern Jewish institutions to make room for women's commitments and styles. It means that we must listen to the views of the others who have been silent or invisible in our tradition. It means that those texts and those institutions will change as they are shaped in response to these different voices.

What would Jewish institutions look like if they were shaped in response to the values that seem to be shared by so many women—balance, intimacy, and empowerment? Already the impact of women has been felt by the men who have been their classmates and colleagues. Rabbi Sher told me that in his view women rabbis have "humanized" male rabbis, that women have taught men about balance. He argues that the definition of success is starting to change as men as well as women are choosing more often to stay in middle-sized congregations, preferring continuity and intimacy and the pleasures of organic growth to the more traditional rewards of prestige and power. These kinds of changes may well change the shape of synagogues, raising new kinds of questions. What would a synagogue look like if success were defined not as climbing to the top of a hierarchy but rather as being at the center of a web of connections? What will careers in the rabbinate look like when maleness is no longer assumed to be the norm, when rabbis are partners rather than seniors and associates, when job sharing is a real possibility, when parental leave is equally accessible to men as to women? What will salaries be like when men as well as women choose to trade some money for more flexible schedules? What will Jewish communities be like when rabbis stop being surrogate Jews and instead enable their communities to take responsibility for their Jewish lives? What will Jewish institutions be like when we make room for the many different kinds of Jews we know there are, Jews in different kinds of families, Jews searching for community and spirituality? And what will the rabbinate be like when we value the diversity among us rabbis: women and men, married and single, lesbian, gay, heterosexual, parents and nonparents, scholars and activists, rabbis who serve in congregations and Hillels and organizations and hospitals and schools...and the list goes on.

These questions of transformation are the most important questions posed by women's rabbinic leadership after twenty years. These are the questions that will shape the next twenty years of our journey. And these are the questions that will lead us out of the wilderness to a Judaism that truly embraces both men and women.

Notes

1. I wish to thank the participants of the Jewish Feminist Research Group of the American Jewish Congress's Jewish Feminist Center (including Professors Tamara Eskensazi and David Ellenson, Rabbis Sue Levi Elwell and Janet Marder, Marcia Spiegel, Diane Schuster, Nurit Shein, Carol Plotkin, Marleen Marks, Linda Thal, Rachel Adler, Yaffa Weisman, and Michele Lenke) for the invaluable discussion about the first draft of this essay. I would also like to thank Rabbis Mark Winer, Debra Hachen, Deborah Prinz, and Arnold Sher for their helpful conversations about these issues and Rabbis Emily Feigenson and Patricia Karlin-Neumann, Professor Judith Resnik, and Ben Bycel for their thoughtful and critical readings of earlier drafts.

2. Carol Gilligan, *In a Different Voice* (Cambridge: Harvard University Press, 1982).

3. Catherine MacKinnon, *Feminism Unmodified* (Cambridge: Harvard University Press, 1987).

An Eye Toward Tomorrow

The Power of God's Voice

Elyse D. Frishman

Where will we be at the fortieth anniversary? That all depends upon how we hear God.

Let us study the first verse of Torah: *"Braishit bara Elohim et hashamayim v'et ha'aretz.* When God began to create the heaven and the earth..." or "In the beginning, God created the heaven and the earth."

The word that precedes "heaven and earth" in Hebrew is *et.* This word, the fourth word of the Torah, has no real meaning. Its sole purpose is to point out the direct object of a sentence. One midrash asks why this word *et*—with no real meaning—is the fourth word of Torah. "In the beginning, God created...nothing"! *Et* is a word with no meaning, a word that only points out the direct object "heaven and earth."

What is this *et*? Perhaps the word suggests that what is on the surface is not obvious; meaning is hidden even where there seems to be no meaning, even when the intent seems to point to something else. Perhaps *et* symbolizes all things; its two letters are the *alef* and the *taf*, suggesting the entire alef-bet: *et* is all-inclusive. So we learn: God created everything at once. But that creation is too much for us, so we perceive it a bit at a time—through heaven and earth.

From the very first verse of Torah we learn: Look beyond the obvious.

Rabbinic Judaism offered a God who was merciful as well as judgmental, gentle as well as angry, forgiving as well as demanding. It is no accident that so many of us still see God as a forbidding sovereign—one whose

83

underlying love and compassion are still overlaid with fear and trembling; a divine being to be looked up to and who necessarily looks down on us; a commander.

Indeed, rabbinic Judaism is based on this God who commands us to act according to the rules of the covenant. These rules are the mitzvah system. But ultimately, as long as we hear God commanding us, this system limits our relationship. How much freedom can we truly have?

Our Reform movement is spiritually deeper today than it was two decades ago. *Tikkun olam* is no longer just an expression of social justice; it suggests personal renewal. Beyond mending the fabric of our world, we are repairing our own souls.

This is an era of spiritual *teshuva*. My children's lives as Reform Jews are radically different from my own childhood as a Reform Jew. When I was in fifth grade, my religious school teacher had us research different creation myths and compare them with our own. It was interesting, an exercise in *cultural* comparison. But my kids study the text of our creation story and understand its *spiritual* message and impact.

We think and talk about God more. Prayer is important to us, and we are conscious of the setting and tools of worship. Work proceeds on a new prayerbook, to be completed by the turn of the century. We debate the role of halakhah in our movement. We struggle to live more Jewishly, to express our spirituality in healing deeds and rituals. And at the core of our growth and evolution is God. We are sensitive to God language; we strive to open our classrooms and sanctuaries to God. But how *do* we relate to God? How do we *hear* God?

We need to ask ourselves honestly: How well *do* we communicate with God? So many people speak of a sense of distance from God–despite the fact that they want to feel closer. Perhaps the problem is not theirs but reflects the limitation of their teachers: the ways in which *we* understand and teach about God.

In Reform Judaism, do we believe that God commands us? In *Gates of Mitzvah*–the title is suggestive–Herman Schaalman wrote about the divine authority of the mitzvah.

God became the...*Metzaveh* because Moses, in his extraordinary nearness to God, thus understood, thus interpreted, thus "heard," the impact and meaning of God's presence. God is *Metzaveh*–Commander–because Moses experienced himself as *metzuveh*–commanded, summoned, directed. And this is why Moses transmitted what he "heard," why he expressed the meaning of God's Presence in the mitzvot, the commandments to the people at Sinai and to their descendants ever after. This is why the Torah is both *Torat Adonai*, God's Torah, and *Torat Mosheh*, Moses' Torah. This is why the Talmud can say–Torah speaks human language.[1]

The Torah speaks to us in human language, but how do we hear God's voice? And how does Torah *reflect* what we have heard?

When we listen to Torah, we are listening to God's voice. But this is not necessarily how God speaks; it is how *we* hear. Dialogue between two people grows not from what is said but from what is heard. Just listen to the conversation between a teenager and parent! Consider how a child may hear a parent speaking in a certain tone and may answer accordingly, while the parent was unaware of that tone. How often are we misunderstood because someone has misperceived our tone?

There are three ways in Torah in which we hear God's voice. Consider these three Hebrew verbs: *dabeir, amar, tzivah*. These are the three means for God to address us in the Torah. We hear God **speaking** to us, as in *"**Vaydabeir** Adonai el Mosheh*; God spoke to Moses." We hear God **saying** something to us, as in *"Vaydabeir Adonai el Mosheh **laymor***; God spoke to Moses, saying." And we hear God **commanding** us, as in *"Ka'asher **tzivah** Adonai el Mosheh*; as God commanded Moses." These are the only three verbal forms of communication between us and God. We need to understand when they are used and the different impacts of each.

There is a marked difference between a relationship that is commanded and one that suggests give-and-take, reflecting a dialogue. Consider how you feel when you are told what to do rather than guided to do something.

In feminist language, **commanding** is hierarchical and **speaking** is relational.

Deborah Tannen, in her important work, *You Just Don't Understand*, distinguishes the ways in which men and women communicate. Men tend to speak hierarchically; women generally talk in a relational manner. By way of illustration, Tannen observes that men rarely interrupt each other in conversation: it is considered rude. Men listen to one other, then pick up when the other has finished. They build their ideas, one on top of the other; the turf is always well-defined. This style is hierarchical. Women, however, interrupt each other all the time. Why? They feed each other's thoughts, intuitively building together until an idea is completed. It matters less who owns the idea than that it exists. This style is called relational.

Consider the three verbs: *dabeir, amar, tzivah*. The first two are relational–God talking with us; the last, *tzivah*, is hierarchical–God commanding us. We can note in Torah that God is never interrupted in the *tzivah* form; but God is even challenged in the *dabeir* and *amar* forms.

When are these different verbs employed? One would think, considering the weight of the mitzvah system, that *tzivah* is the most important and oft-used verb. We should be able to find it in all situations where important instructions are given.

Consider some examples from Genesis, Exodus, and Leviticus.

The first big mitzvah is circumcision.

> God further **said** to Abraham:
> As for you, you and your offspring to come throughout
> the ages shall keep my covenant...
> every male among you shall be circumcised
> ...And when he was done **speaking** with him,
> God was gone from Abraham. Then Abraham...
> circumcised the flesh of their foreskins on that very day,
> as God had **spoken** to him. (Gen. 17)

God does not command Abraham to do circumcision. Indeed, God's words are strongly directive; but Abraham perhaps is impelled to do it because of the strong bond that occurred from their dialogue. How moving that when God finishes speaking with Abraham, Abraham no longer has God's presence with him!

The Ten Commandments are truly *Aseret Dibrot*, the Ten Statements. Read the beginning of Exodus 20: "***Vaydabeir*** Elohim *et kol* **hadvarim** *haeileh* **laymor**...; God spoke all these words, saying..."

> God **spoke** all these words, **saying**:
> I am the Lord your God who brought you out of the land of
> Egypt, the house of bondage:
> you shall have no other gods beside Me. (Exod. 20:1-2)

How did these verses come to be known as the Ten *Commandments*? God isn't *commanding*; God is *instructing, guiding, relating* to us.

The Holiness Code, from Leviticus 19, contains the crucial ethical and ritual guidelines for Jewish living: "***Vaydabeir*** Adonai *el Mosheh* **laymor**...**Dabeir** *el bnai yisrael,* **vamarta** *aleyhem, K'doshem tihyu kee kadosh ani.* God spoke to Moses saying, 'Speak to the Israelites and say to them, "You shall be holy because I, Adonai, am holy."'"

> The Lord **spoke** to Moses **saying**:
> **Speak** to the whole Israelite community and **say** to them:
> You shall be holy, for I, the Lord your God, am holy."
> (Lev. 19:1-2)

In this rich moment we learn that abiding by God's words draws us closer to God, revealing and uplifting our souls. We do not need to be commanded to appreciate this.

The teaching of Kashrut from Leviticus 11: "***Vaydabeir*** Adonai *el Mosheh v'el Aharon* **laymor** *alayhem:* **Dabroo** *el bnai yisrael* **laymor,** *zot hachaya asher tochloo mikol hab'haymah al ha'aretz.* And the Lord **spoke** to Moses and Aaron, **saying** to them: **Speak** to the Israelite people thus: These are the creatures that you may eat from among all the land animals." Note again that the verb *tzivah*—command—is not used.

Whenever God addresses us about something important, God *speaks* to us. In personal communication to Abraham or Rebecca or Miriam or

Moses, we hear God with the stronger verb *dabeir*. When we hear God speaking in a softer tone, one-on-one, *amar* is used. When our people hear God, first God *m'dabier*—speaks—then God *omeir*—says.

Where do we find the use of *tzivah*? It has both human and divine usage. Rebecca commands Jacob: "*V'atah bni, shema b'koli la'asher ani* **m'tzavah** *otach*. Now, my son, listen to me while I **command** you." Isaac instructs Jacob not to marry a Canaanite woman, "***Vay'tzaveihoo*** *va'yomeir lo...*; and he **commanded** him, saying..."

In human usage, the intent involves control: "Do what I say without questioning!" But how is the term used between God and people? Intriguingly, women of Torah never hear God "commanding"; when the entire assembly of men and women gather to hear God's words, only the verbs *dabeir* and *omeir* are used.

Examine these well-known verses from Exodus: "*Vayavo Mosheh vaysapeir l'am et kol **divrei** Adonai/ v'et kol ha'mishpatim/ vaya'an kol ha'am/ kol echad/ **Vayomeir**: kol had'varim asher **dibeir** Adonai naaseh.*

> Moses went and repeated to the people
> all the **words** of the Lord and all the rules:
> and all the people answered with one voice, **saying**:
> All the things which the Lord has **spoken** of we will do!
> (Exod. 24:3)

"*Vayikach sefer habrit/vayikra b'oznai ha'am/ **vayomroo**: kol asheir **dibeir** Adonai naaseh v'nishma.*

> Then he took the record of the covenant and read it
> aloud to the people. And they **said**:
> All that the Lord has **spoken**, we will do and understand!
> (Exod. 24:7)

Our ancestral mothers and fathers affirmed their commitment to God's words. Notice that they do not hear God commanding them. They do hear God's voice speaking to them, and they want to respond, to follow through and understand. The mystical moment of feeling close to God is sufficient motivation. We do not need to be commanded to want to live Jewishly.

Only when the assembly is lacking women does the verb *tzivah* appear. Our matriarchs and Miriam never heard God as a commander. Though they had powerful conversations with or about God, never was there this controlling verb. Why?

We return to Deborah Tannen's study. Men and women do dialogue—and hear—differently. The words may be the same, but the method of communication is not.

We, too, do not hear God commanding us. What a relief to recognize that not only is *tzivah* less employed than we thought, but it is never a primary verb in the most significant interactions between us and God.

Words of Torah hold deep meaning. Whatever difficulties appear in the text reflect the concerns of the beholder. Each revolutionary generation has confronted Torah with its own particular concerns. The rabbis arduously worked to reconcile such problems as *"V'hac'na'a'ni az b'aretz;* the Canaanites were then in the land."* Scholars of biblical criticism tackled the discrepancy of the numbers of animals on Noah's ark. And our generation? We embrace choice. So we read Torah and we hear God's voice speaking to us in a different tone. Does the Torah text substantiate autonomy? Yes.

God addresses us primarily in a relationship, not as a commander. What has come to be known as a body of mitzvot were initially gifts, words to guide and direct our lives meaningfully, spiritually.

Certainly some Jews need to hear God commanding; this is the orthodox system. But many of us do not. We listen to God as a still, small voice, a voice that beckons to us. As our spiritual eyes envision more, our desire to love Jewishly deepens.

The biblical God addressed us in relational language. There was a strong bond, a spoken bond. This bond changed with the rabbis. They needed to assert authority in a time of great upheaval. Their mitzvah system is deliberately hierarchical. Torah gives consequences for not following God's word. We can accept this idea of covenant, of give and take or cause and effect, which binds any serious relationship, interpersonally or with God. But when the rabbis developed the mitzvah system, they developed it *as* men,

primarily *for* men. Reform Judaism is wholly egalitarian; we have helped
our faith's expressions to evolve further because of this perspective. Perhaps now we can understand the "maleness" of a *Metzaveh* and appreciate
why it should not dominate in a Judaism that highlights both men and
women.

What is our motivation if we are not commanded? If we are close to
God, we will abide by the covenant. It is crucial, therefore, that our spiritual lives be strong. Reform Judaism must continue this involvement in the
life of the soul. Consider the impact this involvement has on our prayers. If
our spiritual growth is essential for us to feel bound to God, prayer is a
primary component. Yet how often do we say words that we do not really
mean?

Recall the standard formula for a blessing: *"asher kidshanu b'mitzvotav
vitzivanu*...who has made us holy with His commandments, and commanded
us to..." We have seen that God *has* made us holy in Torah but has drawn
us near simply by speaking with us. I do not light Shabbat candles because
I feel commanded. Rather, I feel a sanctity in that moment that draws me
to God. Our prayer language, especially in our most basic formula blessings, should reflect this departure from hierarchical thinking.

The last paragraph of the *V'ahavta* says that we should *remember* and
do all God's *commandments*. It is fascinating how our Reform liturgists
collapsed several intervening paragraphs as anachronistic but kept this section that specifically calls upon us to follow all of God's commands. We do
not support this idea. It is cognitively dissonant for us to say it. Why do
we?

The words of our liturgy must reflect courageously our theology. As
we view Torah with new spiritual and feminine insights, we should revise
these words. Our prayerbook already reflects a range of theologies: the
Gates of Prayer offers so many options, and the new gender-sensitive version acknowledges previous limitations.[2] But we need to go further,
exploring the very essence of our siddur, its language and format, the mes-
sages and concepts it conveys to women and men about how we hear God
and communicate with God.

One decade from now brings us into the new century. People tend to get messianic at such times. For our movement, there will be new leadership in every facet: our seminary, the Union of American Hebrew Congregations, and the Central Conference of American Rabbis; we will have a new prayerbook; and many of our children will be grown and grandchildren will have been born.

In the beginning, God created *et*; God gave us mystery. What seems obvious may not be so. It may seem that Judaism is a mitzvah-based system; but perhaps it is not. The rabbis created this impression with good intent. *We* are of a different generation, one that hears God differently—for our own survival as Jews. The Torah supports our *hearing* of the text.

We crave God's presence. We hear God's voice. Let us not push God away because we do not feel commanded. Let us embrace the God who speaks with us. And may the words of our mouths reflect the meditations of our hearts, that our souls may rise ever higher.

Notes

1. Simeon J. Maslin, ed., *Gates of Mitzvah: A Guide to the Jewish Life Cycle* (New York: Central Conference of American Rabbis, 1979).

2. Chaim Stern, ed., *Gates of Prayer: The New Union Prayerbook* (New York: Central Conference of American Rabbis, 1975).

Transformation of the Rabbinate:

Future Directions and Prospects

David Ellenson

Jewish tradition is replete with legends and tales. Each generation re-
ceives, creates, and transmits still more stories and, in providing such
narratives, helps to forge meaning, identity, and linkages for generations
past, present, and future. Community emerges out of stories, as do moral
and religious visions. We now celebrate a new chapter in the ongoing story
of Judaism—twenty years of women being ordained as rabbis among and
for the people Israel. It is appropriate, as we ponder the meaning and
significance of this novel development in our people's history, and as we
reflect upon what the meaning of this story will be for a future generation,
to return to an ancient and puzzling legend of our people, one that I believe can instruct us in our deliberations today.

"*Tanu rabbanan*; our rabbis taught," are the familiar words with which
this talmudic tale from Shabbat 53b begins. The story continues: "It once
happened that a man's wife died and left a child to be suckled, and he
could not afford to pay a wet nurse, whereupon a miracle was performed
for him and his nipples opened like the two nipples of a woman and he
suckled his son. Rabbi Joseph observed, 'Come and see how great was this
man that a miracle was performed on his account.' Said Abaye to him,
'How despicable [*garu-a*] was this man that the order of creation was
changed on his account." Rashi, the exegete par excellence of the Jewish

93

tradition, in commenting upon this passage, observes that *garu-a*, as employed by Abaye in his description of the miracle wrought for this man and his son, should be translated as "lowly," for the man's impoverished state prevented him from hiring a wet nurse to suckle his motherless child. However, as with all stories and legends, other interpretations are surely plausible and, as my own translation indicates, perhaps more appropriate for deriving meaning from the text that is relevant to our purposes.

Unlike Rashi, I would suggest that Abaye's perspective on this father and the miracle performed on his behalf must be viewed as more than a simple commentary on the man's financial state. After all, as Rashi himself observes, elsewhere in the Talmud Abaye looks upon the performance of a miracle on an individual's behalf as a sign of divine grace. Why, we may ask, does this act in our story not adduce similar approbation on Abaye's part? The answer, it seems to me, lies in rabbinic tradition's strict definitions of gender roles. Abaye, in labeling this man *garu-a*, is driven to such anger because the strict sense of order and the boundaries that mark his world are dependent upon the routinization of sex functions and gender roles. The comprehensibility and predictability of the social order have been violated through this act of grace bestowed upon the father. The father's being miraculously blessed and empowered with the ability to sustain and nurture his son in this way has violated sexual demarcations that Abaye regards as essential for the world to be intelligible. Abaye has internalized these demarcations as not just appropriate but inviolate in defining the universe. This particular alteration in the natural order of sexual function, unlike other miracles, appears to enrage him precisely because it threatens to plunge the world of daily living, everyday life, into chaos. As such, it must be deplored.

Echoes of this attitude about sexual roles abound in the writings of rabbinic tradition. A modern example can be found in a responsum of the late Rabbi Moshe Feinstein. Rabbi Feinstein, when queried in 1976 about the inroads feminism was making in the Orthodox community, noted that some groups of Orthodox women (*shomrot torah*) desired to carry into the realm of Jewish law the "war" that feminists in the outside world were waging against traditionally assigned gender roles. Such intrusions and attempts at transformation and change, Rabbi Feinstein felt, were totally inappropriate and illegitimate. Judaism, he wrote, was based upon the principle that all of the Torah, both written and oral, was given by God to Moses at Sinai. Later generations of Jews therefore possessed no right to change even a single element in God's eternal and revealed law. While the rationale for some precepts of Torah are unknown, the reasons for the domestic role assigned by Jewish tradition to women are "clear to everyone; *giluyim lakol.*" It is obvious, according to Rabbi Feinstein, that in the very act of creating the world, God assigned specific roles to each sex in the animal kingdom. The task God designated for the female sex was that of raising children, and humankind is no exception to this law of nature. Women are more suited than men for the performance of this domestic task. The rabbis, aware of this truth, legislated a domestic role for women. Social conventions and domestic arrangements may be transformed in the larger world. Men may desire domestic roles and women public ones. Nevertheless, the Torah of God is eternal (*nitzhit*), and one who would transform gender roles is engaged in a struggle against God and the order of nature as God ordained it. From Abaye through Rabbi Feinstein, one Jewish attitude toward the role women properly ought to render in society is maintained.[1] For women to suggest or engage in a role that questions traditional boundaries placed around the sacred is to challenge more than the social construction of gender. It is, as Abaye put it, to alter the "order of creation."

Furthermore, we would be naive and mistaken to assume that it has been only the world of traditional rabbinic Judaism that has insisted upon the maintenance of these gender roles and boundaries. Traditional Judaism has not been alone in defending the public prerogative of the male sex. Every patriarchally constructed society and institution has socialized its members into accepting this sexual division of labor as correct and proper. As Riv-Ellen Prell has demonstrated, the Reform movement, despite its proclamation of the religious equality of men and women as early as the 1840s, rendered women "invisible in the public realm" and over 125 years lapsed between the declaration of the religious equality of men and women and the ordination of Sally Priesand in 1972.[2]

The decision to ordain women as rabbis, to have them engage in public roles of religious leadership within the Jewish community, must thus be
considered revolutionary. The ordination of women as rabbis has brought
into focus the dynamics of a gendered religious life that has both silenced
women's voices and muted feminist values of cooperation, mutuality, and
equality. It has spoken directly to the reality of how power is gendered as
well as conceptualized within our community and its traditions. As Paula
Hyman has observed: "Gender is not merely about social and culturally
defined differences between the sexes. It is also a primary way of signifying
relationships of power."[3] In electing to ordain Sally Priesand as rabbi, the
Reform movement broke with the past. The significance of this act should
not be underestimated, and the novel presence of women in the rabbinate,
like other transformative moments in the history of Judaism, grants us
ample reason to celebrate today. The reasons for celebration are many.

CAUSES FOR CELEBRATION

"*Dibrah Torah kilshon b'nei adam*. The Torah," our tradition asserts,
"speaks in human language." The variegated languages employed to express the truths of Torah, as well as the institutional patterns that are
established to express those truths, are internalized in the minds and hearts
of Jews in every generation who adhere to and identify with tradition. These
religious truths, superimposed as they are on life, shape the deepest ways
we envision and experience the reality of the world. The ordination of
women as rabbis is potentially so transformative precisely because it breaks
with gendered patterns of image, power, and role bequeathed from the
past. The emergence of women in the rabbinate has provided and continues to provide new paradigms for how the present and future may be
experienced and understood by Jews. By establishing an ideal of gender
equality in the public roles and private lives of Jews, this decision has altered the character of our community in ways that would have been
unthinkable twenty years ago.

An anecdote illustrating the nature of this change concerns an incident
involving my wife Jackie nearly a decade ago, when she served as a rabbi in
a suburban Los Angeles congregation. One day a mother of one of the

kindergarten children showed Jackie a picture that her daughter had drawn in school. It was a drawing, the little girl had told the mother, of God. What made such a pictorial representation of the deity unusual was that, in this instance, God was not depicted as an elderly gentleman with a beard. Instead, God was wearing a skirt. When the mother asked her child why she envisaged God in this manner, the little girl replied, "This is how the rabbi looks."

Such a story is significant precisely because it is not unique to my wife. Other women rabbis relate similar, if not identical, incidents. The childhood images children in such stories possess of God as female undoubtedly open up the possibility that in their adult years many Jews will envision the divine, to use Judith Plaskow's felicitous phrase, as something besides "Dominating Other." The very theological foundation of God's maleness upon which so much of Judaism is established is challenged by the appearance of women in the pulpit. The story testifies to the ineffability of God and the mystery and infinity of all religious symbols and how penultimate they are in their plausibility. Most important, the presence of women in the pulpit instructs all Jews that God is beyond all word and cannot be contained by insisting upon the masculinity of the divine.

Furthermore, the ordination of women as rabbis has granted some women access to other positions of religious authority in the community that had been denied them in the past. Dr. Deborah Cohen, a physician in Los Angeles, reports that despite her upbringing as a Reform Jew in Long Island in the 1960s, it never occurred to her that women could serve as religious functionaries. However, after listening to a speech delivered by Rabbi Laura Geller, she recognized that it was possible for women to serve in such a capacity. As a result, she approached the Reform movement to initiate a program that would train both female and male physicians as *mohalim* and *mohalot*. Due to her persistence—and the scholarly and organizational leadership provided by Rabbi Lewis Barth—there are now dozens of Reform women and men throughout the United States who have been educated and certified by the Reform movement as *mohalim* and *mohalot*. The decision to ordain women as rabbis, and the appearance of women in other roles of religious leadership as a result of this decision, have contributed directly to a more inclusionary style of leadership in Jewish life for both men and women than would have been possible had women not been ordained as rabbis.

Moreover, the decision to ordain women as rabbis has meant that the ritual and liturgical life of the Jewish community has been opened to the possibilities of change unprecedented in the contemporary era. The authorship of gender-inclusive prayerbooks informed by the tenets of feminist Judaism is a challenge large sectors of the non-Orthodox community now uncontestably regard as a legitimate enterprise. Surely the next twenty years will see many more efforts in this direction. The bat mitzvah ceremony is universally observed now in liberal Jewish congregations, and the *simhat bat* ceremony is well on its way to similar inclusion. Rituals marking moments in the life cycle that were formerly ignored–from miscarriage through birth, from weaning to the onset of menstruation and menopause–are now in the process of creation.[4] Other changes of this type that affect the lives of both Jewish men and Jewish women could readily be cited. Furthermore, these changes are witnessed both in noninstitutionalized and traditional denominational settings. The appearance of women in the pulpit has surely promoted, and will certainly continue to stimulate, these innovations.

All the achievements enumerated thus far are real. They bespeak the impact of women's entry into the rabbinate and are indicative of a direction the community is more and more likely to take as children reared on the ideal of gender equality and provided with the example of strong women in public roles reach adulthood. In this sense, there is no question that the appearance of women in the rabbinate is revolutionary and subversive of traditional Judaism. It constitutes, as have other innovative moments in the Jewish past, an act, in Gershon Shaked's words, of "creative betrayal," a moment when ideals and cultural forms present within the larger host culture are incorporated into the religious and national life of the Jewish people.

The changes I have described and celebrated up to this point were and are based upon a liberal ideal that affirms that women and men share a common human nature that endows both sexes with identical social and natural rights. From such premises the conclusion follows that equal rights and opportunities ought to be granted to all members of society. Simple justice demands that equal opportunity be extended to all members of society regardless of gender. These liberal assumptions have unquestionably succeeded in opening up the rabbinate to women and in raising the realities and possibilities for transformation enumerated above. In short, this liberal ideal and model has secured for women the right to ordination. It has simultaneously made us aware of the "glass ceiling" that marks virtually every area of our institutional lives. Much remains to be done. While recent years have seen the addition of women to the faculty of Hebrew Union College-Jewish Institute of Religion, more women—particularly ordained women—need to be hired. The curriculum should be formally expanded to include women's studies or feminist concerns. Issues such as sexual harassment or female rabbinic placement should be more sufficiently addressed. Lack of salary parity for women who perform the same tasks as their male counterparts in the congregational rabbinate is an egregious wrong that cries out for remedy. Our affirmation of the truth of the liberal ideals enumerated above and our belief that these ideals are at the heart of and are accommodated within the best of Jewish religious tradition demand that we examine and act upon all these matters as we confront the next twenty years.

These commitments and affirmations also compel us to face other questions that transcend the liberal commitments that have brought us to this moment. They force us to ask how the presence of women in the rabbinate will transform, as other comparably novel moments have, the nature of the rabbinate, the synagogue, and Judaism itself. Will the appearance of women in the rabbinate simply indicate that traditional Judaism has extended itself so as to provide "equal access" to women in the variegated arenas of Jewish life? If the latter alone is true, and if, in view of the tasks I have enumerated above, this dream of equal access can be realized, it is surely no mean feat, and we, schooled in the canons of Western liberalism, should applaud these accomplishments. However, in considering the future impact of women in the rabbinate, the prospects of what more this decision might mean should also be considered. It is with these thoughts in mind that I turn to the final considerations of this essay.

REVOLUTIONARY PROSPECTS

Rabbi Tracy Guren Klirs, in speaking of the ritual transformations that have marked contemporary Jewish life as a result of the appearance of women's voices and concerns in the public life of Judaism, has written: "Steps [such as the ones I have described] are merely ameliorative. They do not begin to affect what many see as the fundamentally patriarchal nature of the classic rabbinic tradition, of Jewish theology, of Torah itself. Women did not have a hand in forming these traditions, and so women's experiences have been left out of them. For women to be fully included in normative Jewish liturgy and practice and to be truly valued by the entire Jewish community, it will be necessary for them to create new traditions which reflect their experiences and include their unique spiritual insights."[5]

Rabbi Klirs reminds us that the religious and cultural forms, the patriarchal assumptions that have supported and defined traditional Judaism, including the rabbinate, are to be questioned, amended, supplemented, and possibly redefined in light of feminist concerns and consciousness. This is the issue that most seriously and radically confronts us as we deal with the question of how the presence of women rabbis will challenge and possibly change the future of the rabbinate, congregational life, and the Jewish community itself twenty years from now. It is an issue that few male leaders foresaw when the decision was made to grant women equal access to the rabbinate two decades ago.

Prophecy, as the Talmud informs us, is no longer a Jewish gift. The enterprise of offering predictions is clearly a hazardous one. The directions the Jewish story will take as a result of women in the rabbinate cannot yet be fully appreciated or defined, precisely because we have not yet seen what the parameters and contours of this new chapter will be. A definitive answer to the questions and musings of this essay is impossible to give. Thus, I offer some final thoughts as prescriptions, hopes that reflect the directions in which I believe the Jewish community and the Reform movement ought to move as a result of women in the rabbinate. In order to offer such prescriptions, we must ask what a feminist orientation in the world might be. Such an orientation will help us envision how a Judaism, a synagogue, and a community informed by these principles might appear.

In so doing, we must also ponder how, in light of these feminist principles of transformation, the integrity of the Jewish story might be maintained.

The myth of Persephone is well known to all of us. Persephone, the beautiful daughter of Demeter, the goddess of agriculture and fertility, was kidnapped and seized by Hades, god of the underworld, who desired Persephone on account of her beauty. Demeter was heartbroken by this loss, and she wandered the earth looking for her daughter. When Demeter discovered the fate that had befallen Persephone, she was furious and demanded that Zeus retrieve her daughter from the clutches of Hades and return Persephone to her mother. Persephone, heartsick at her absence from her mother, was anxious to return. Tragically, she had eaten some seeds from a pomegranate while living in the underworld and was thus, according to the tale, unable to return permanently to her mother Demeter. Zeus arranged a compromise. For eight months each year, Persephone would depart the underworld and dwell with her mother; the remaining months of the year would be spent in the underworld with Hades. During the period that Persephone dwelt with Demeter, Demeter was overjoyed and warmth and fertility marked the earth. However, when Persephone returned to Hades, Demeter was beside herself with grief and winter ensued, the earth becoming cold and barren.

This tale, commonly cited as an explanation for the changes in season, is much more than that. It is, as many have pointed out, the archetypical feminist myth. Primacy is accorded in this story to the relationship that occurs between Demeter and her daughter Persephone. It is a myth that sees the worth of the individual as expressed most fully only in response to another. The notion of the autonomous individual as the highest expression of the moral self—an ideal that has long dominated both classical and modern trends in Western philosophy—is here dislodged in favor of a moral vision that sees reciprocity and responsiveness in relationships as the most appropriate and ethically compelling vision of what it means to be human. Attachment is preferred to detachment, connection to separation. Mutual dependence is seen as possessing a greater moral valence than an atomizing individuality. The myth of Persephone provides an alternative moral vision, an ethical corrective, to the excessive individualism that has heretofore so dominated our Western vision of a mature and appropriate morality.

The vision of Persephone promotes an image of self in relationship that views community, the self standing in relationship to and engaged in dialogue with others, as the central fact of moral life. The self comes to be defined in interactions with others and, in so doing, is open to the possibility of transformation that responsiveness in human engagement offers. The individual stands in a state of mutual interdependence with others, and relationships are sustained and nurtured through attention and response. As one anonymous person, commenting upon such a vision, has observed, moral responsibility does not thus signify a Kantian notion of "an internalized conscience enacted by will and guided by duty or obligation." Instead, it means being "aware of others and...of their feelings...Responsibility is taking charge of yourself by looking at others around you and seeing what they need and what you need...and taking the initiative." The traditional concept of autonomy, as Carol Gilligan has pointed out, is not wholly abandoned in such a vision. It is, however, unmistakably altered. The individual is not separate, nor are relationships essentially either hierarchical or contractual. The self stands in connection with others and is "defined by gaining voice and perspective known in the experience of engagement with others." Being dependent in such a vision "no longer means being helpless, powerless, and without control; it signifies a conviction that one is able to have an effect on others, as well as the recognition that the interdependence of attachment empowers both the self and the other, not one person at the other's expense."[6]

Dialogue and response replace reflection and abstract commitment to principle. Such a potentially communitarian ethic is a compelling one at a time when tribalization, conflict, and isolation have so dominated and diminished national, religious, and ethnic life in the world and the nation as well as among our own people. A consciousness of that ethic is among the great gifts that feminism and feminist theory have bestowed upon us. The ordination of women as rabbis has helped grant this vision an audience among contemporary Jews that will ultimately enrich the entire community and allow us self-consciously to direct our energies into the creation of a Jewish community that is marked as much by care and compassion as it is by an abstract and impersonal commitment to duties and rules. Such an orientation is, in a very real sense, critical of certain aspects of traditional Judaism. It indicates that those elements within the tradition that have been employed to subordinate others—particularly women—in the name of abstract and putatively divine laws must be attacked as unauthentic and oppressive. Few liberal Jews would, I presume, dissent from this stance. After all, much of Reform Judaism can be construed as offering a comparable critique of elements of rabbinic tradition.

The crucial issue is whether a call for a feminist approach to Judaism that emphasizes the relational dimensions of the tradition in a non-hierarchical way is one that can be harmonized with the past. Or, to use the language employed earlier in this presentation, can the integrity of the Jewish story be maintained if the narrative, personal elements of the tradition are assigned a weight and authority they seemingly did not possess in earlier times? These questions, from my own perspective, are largely rhetorical—for the feminist ethic I have described is one that is thoroughly consistent with the primary thrust of biblical and rabbinic tradition. The Book of Ruth provides a classical warrant for this type of thought within biblical Judaism and assures us that an affirmation of a relational model of ethics is at the core of Jewish tradition.

As my friend Rabbi Patricia Karlin-Neumann pointed out to me in a recent conversation, the first chapter of Ruth is a story of relationship. Viewed from a feminist perspective, one sees in the initial chapter that Naomi, after the death of her husband and her sons, feels bereft and isolated, alone in the world. It is the devotion and care shown to her by Ruth, Ruth's insistence on the bond of relationship that links Naomi to her, that brings Naomi from the realm of solitude and mourning back into life. When Ruth, despite the insistent pleadings of her mother-in-law that she return to Moab, asserts, "Entreat me not to leave you, or to return from following after you, for where you go, I will go; and where you lodge, I will lodge, your people shall be my people, and your God my God. Where you die, I will die, and there I will be buried," she displays a feminist sensibility that acknowledges that attachments are irreplaceable. Ruth's attachment to her husband and her love for Naomi cannot be forgotten, and they find expression in the present affirmations she offers her mother-in-law.

Furthermore, the obligations that Ruth then takes upon herself are not abstract constructs imposed upon her in a vacuum. They are duties that emerge out of the tranformative capacities of human relationship.

If one looks to the Bible and the writings of the rabbis as "historical prototypes" that provide us "with a sense of [our] ongoing history as well as [our] theological identity,"[7] this interpretation of Ruth indicates that the feminist ethic of which we have spoken is embedded in the historical narratives of our people. It reminds us that all the abstract duties imposed upon us by our tradition are ultimately embedded in a story that speaks of our people's relationship with the divine, and it reminds us that the rules imposed by that tradition are ultimately expressions of and thus subservient to a broader ideal of covenantal partnership that bestows ultimate meaning upon our actions and upon our attempts to forge community. The feminist ethos I have described, far from being a break with the tradition, ultimately embodies the tradition's most noble sentiments—albeit with some different emphases. In this sense, the feminist ethos described in these closing remarks is akin to the sentiments expressed about Jewish religiosity in our century by Martin Buber, the great philosopher of dialogue whose influence upon contemporary liberal Judaism has been immense.

The challenge that remains is whether this ethic of compassion, care, and relationship will ultimately find the expression it deserves in our institutions. Much needs to be done to see that the agenda of egalitarianism is fully realized and achieved over the next twenty years. Even more challenging, however, is the degree to which we will be able to forge community in our institutions and congregations and transform these entities as well as ourselves and our families into caring persons, places, and units that provide the support and nurturance heralded by a feminist and Jewish ethos.

This transformation can only be done if we have the courage to go beyond the rhetoric of this ethos and implant it in the lives of rabbis, the rabbinate, and the institutions we serve. The life-style of the rabbinate and the work ethic that has traditionally accompanied it must be transformed. How can we, who are supposed to provide care and nurturance for others and model compassion for our communities, do so if the professional demands of a seemingly endless work week preclude us from spending time with our families? How can we provide the responsiveness our vocation legitimately requires if we are too exhausted by the demands of work? How can we speak of the integrity, beauty, and warmth of the Jewish home and family, the importance of community the synagogue and the Jewish federations provide, if we do not understand that the personal dimension of our lives is foremost and must be the anchor from which we draw our strength and the integrity of our institutional direction? The "personal is political" is by now a time-worn slogan of the feminist movement. Yet it remains vital. It reminds us that these two realms of life are not separate from one another but are distinct parts of an overarching whole.

The feminization of the rabbinate introduced by the Hebrew Union College-Jewish Institute of Religion twenty years ago when Rabbi Alfred Gottschalk ordained Sally Priesand a rabbi among the people Israel means more than the appearance of women in the pulpit, alterations in the liturgy, creations of new rituals, and the discovery and expression of women's voices in both the history and the ongoing public life of our people. Of course, it means all those things. However, it points to much more. It asks us to create the wholeness promised by the ethic of relationship in both our personal and our communal lives. It points to the possibility that rabbinical positions in the Jewish community will be shared so that rabbis can practice the family and communal ethos about which they so eloquently preach. It points to the possibility that a laity will be educated to understand and appreciate that their rabbis are not their servants who are at their beck and call at every moment for any reason nor are their rabbis their superiors who dictate the essence and practice of Judaism to and for them. Instead, the feminization of the rabbinate points to rabbis who are their partners, persons knowledgeable of and trained in the Jewish tradition who are prepared and delighted to grant their congregants access to the wisdom, insights, ethics, rituals, and spirituality inherent in Judaism. This transformation does not mean the demise of large congregations. Nor does it signal the necessity of small ones. Instead, it calls for the restructuring of our institutions so that intimacy and support can be provided through a myriad of programs and by a variety of persons for the care and nurturance of our beleaguered and tired, yet ever hopeful and optimistic, people. This is the revolutionary potential that the ordination of the women has released.

In the beginning of this essay, I cited the famous passage from Shabbat 53b and Abaye's outrage at the miracle that allowed the anonymous man to nurse his motherless child. I also recognize that many women, commenting upon this passage, have viewed it as just one more instance in which the male authors of the text claim for men biological functions of which they are normally deprived and, in so doing, rob women of their uniqueness. Undoubtedly there is more than a modicum of fairness in this critique. However, in light of the analysis I have presented, I would like to offer yet one more commentary—this one focusing upon the remarks of Rabbi Joseph and the contrast they present to the words of Abaye.

When Rabbi Joseph asserts, "how great is this man," I like to think he is proclaiming that divinity is ultimately found in the ability to nurture and sustain, in the loving bonds that result from the intimacy of relationship and compassion that is literally embodied in the act of nursing. Abaye's outrage about this miracle stemmed, in part, from the fear he felt because of the unknown meaning and outcome of this act. Today, too, others are outraged, and perhaps fearful, of the portraits of transformation and potential for change outlined at this conference. Yet Rabbi Joseph, unlike Abaye, understood and had the courage to affirm the ultimate truth—the Jewish truth—this story expresses. The future, of course, is unknown, and many Jews, like Abaye, are afraid of what it holds. That fear may well prevent the promises I have discussed here from becoming reality.

As we look forward to the next two decades, may we have the courage to dissent from Abaye and affirm the wisdom of Rabbi Joseph. May the presence of women in the rabbinate mean that all Jews—men as well as women—strive to create intimate moments and settings within both our private lives and our institutions where an ethic of care within a framework of relationships will find increasing expression. This would represent the promise of transformation already heralded by the appearance of women in the rabbinate. It would mean the increasing fulfillment of the messianic promise that lies at the heart of our religion.

Notes

1. *Iggerot Moshe, Orah Hayyim* 4:49.

2. Riv-Ellen Prell, "The Dilemma of Women's Equality in Reform Judaism," *Judaism* 30 (Fall 1981): 418-26.

3. Paula Hyman, "Gender and Identity in Modern Jewish History, *Masoret* 2, no. 1 (Fall 1992): 9. (*Masoret* is a publication of the Jewish Theological Seminary.)

4. Elana Zaiman, then a fifth-year rabbinical student at the Jewish Theological Seminary of America, and now a Rabbi at Park Avenue Synagogue in New York, has testified to this development in her article, "Grappling with 'Tradition and Change'" in ibid., 8.

5. Tracy Guren Klirs, *The Merit of Our Mothers* (Cincinnati: Hebrew Union College Press, 1992), 10.

6. Carol Gilligan, "Remapping the Moral Domain: New Images of Self in Relationship," in *Mapping the Moral Domain*, edited by Carol Gilligan, Janie Victoria Ward, and Jill McLean Taylor, with Betty Bardige (Cambridge: Harvard University Press, 1988), 3-19; quotes from pp. 6, 7, 17, 16.

7. The language here is taken from Elizabeth Shussler-Fiorenza, *In Memory of Her* (New York: Crossroad, 1984), 33-34.

A Visit to the Future

Nancy Fuchs-Kreimer

"How will women rabbis change the future of the rabbinate, congregational life, and the Jewish community?" The letter from the organizers of this symposium lies before me on my desk. How does one foretell the future? While visiting my parents in California I could consult the Yellow Pages and discover a variety of professionals who can tell me what will be. Alas, divination is forbidden in Leviticus 19:31 and Deuteronomy 18:10-11. The hour is late, the word processor is humming, the screen is blank.

My last thought as I fall asleep over my keyboard: What a solitary, "male" process this is—writing papers for conferences! The next thing I know, I am in Israel. I am journeying to Endor, near Gilboa, with two friends to see the medium—sometimes called a witch—whom Saul consulted in distress before his battle. When I explain to her that I have to speak at the Hebrew Union College in New York City, she understands immediately that, like Saul, I face a great challenge. She prepares a meal for us of fatted calf and unleavened bread.

"You brought up Samuel from the dead to tell him what the future held. Would you be so kind as to bring someone up for us?"

"Who would you like?" she asks.

I debate the options with my friends. We want a Jewish woman from the past to take us on a guided tour of the Jewish future. She should be strong and decisive. We know women rabbis do not *necessarily* mean the triumph of a feminist vision. But we have not come all the way to Endor to see women in navy blue suits carrying bulging briefcases onto commuter trains. We know that it is possible that women will assimilate to male models, that as women leave the realm of home from which their distinctive voice has emerged they will lose that voice as well, that their presence in the rabbinate will mean business as usual. But we want our risen ancestor to show us what things might look like if what is deepest and best in feminism is given a chance to influence the whole. We want to be shown the possible, perhaps the utopian—but in any case, a vision.[1]

We need someone who did not merely assist the flow of sacred history, but who altered the story. We think of Rebecca or Tamar or Judith or Esther, yet we reject them for a better choice. We are women who want to change Judaism together with other women.[2] So we choose Yocheved who, working with her daughter and the Egyptian princess, changed the course of Jewish history.

No sooner have we made our request than we see an old woman wrapped in a robe coming up from the earth. We bow and she asks, "Why have you disturbed me?"

I answer: "I need a vision of the future. I need to know how it is all going to look in twenty years if..."

"If what?"

"If women are true to themselves, if we act with courage, if we get to make a difference—the way you did."

Yocheved smiles. "Since you put it that way, come with me and I will take you on a guided tour of the future *if.*"

EVEN GOD CANNOT CHANGE HISTORY

A moment later we are in a synagogue library filled with magazines, journals, books for adults and children. Yocheved appears on top of a huge pile of newly published books and says with great dramatic effect, "*The first thing that looks different in the Jewish future is the Jewish past.*"

As we begin to leaf through the materials, we realize that the old adage "even God cannot change history" may need some rethinking. We plunge into the stories we never knew, some recovered by historians, others invented by midrashists, all giving us a fuller vision of the Jewish past and both the suffering and the triumphs of Jewish women.

Yocheved is pleased to notice that some of the haggadot are now telling the story of Miriam: "After all those fathers and sons in the Torah, it's about time they honored a mother and daughter pair!" Honor, however belated, is finally being accorded. Even the title page of Louis Ginzberg's Genizah Studies now bears Henrietta Szold's name as well.[3]

Many books have been revised so that the language is gender neutral. But some have been left to stand because, it appears, "man" really meant "humans" and sometimes it really meant "man." I am interested to notice that one of my favorite essays from rabbinical school, "The Lonely Man of Faith" by Soloveitchik, is *still* "The Lonely Man of Faith." But I notice it is now bound in a volume with other essays on the phenomenology of traditional Jewish practice, including one entitled "The Networked Woman of Ritual."

A Different View of Difference

We leave the library and go into the sanctuary. Three rabbis are on the bimah—two men and a woman. They are standing in front of the ark with arms raised for the priestly benediction, symbolic representatives of the divine. But, back in the past where we come from, God was imagined as male by most Jews. We wondered: What does the inclusivity in the rabbinate do to people's image of God?

"People in the future have a choice," Yocheved tells us. They either must conclude that spiritual leaders are not God's representatives, at least not in the way they had thought, or that God looks different at different times."

"What do they decide?"

"Both. Jews are much clearer now than they ever were that the reason we are forbidden from making an image of God is that there are already images of God—every human being on this earth. Seeing women rabbis helps them remember that rabbis are not God figures, any more than any human being is. So, most often, people bless one another in synagogue.

"Sometimes, however, people do crave holy men and women just as they crave holy space and holy time. So, the priestly benediction still gets used on occasion. In the future, people reenter the mythic world with more comfort than in your day. The variety of holy people encourages a variety of ways to imagine the Source of Life."

The multiple images of God, in turn, help affirm a theology of inclusion of all Jews. And just in time! At the same time as women were entering the rabbinate, the Jewish community was becoming more ethnically heterogeneous due to intermarriage, conversion, adoption, new reproductive technologies. If leaders could look different from each other, beginning with gender but extending to other realms, then what is being affirmed is difference. Indeed, as we get closer, we can see those three rabbis on the bimah include one Asian and one person in a wheelchair.

"*The second thing that looks different in the Jewish future*," Yocheved says, "*is Jews*." God, religious leaders, and Jewish people all are celebrated in their variety, and the three celebrations reinforce one another.

THE LESBIAN CONTINUUM

Speaking of difference, let us get back to those three rabbis up there on the bimah doing their priestly benediction. Who are they blessing anyway? They are blessing two Jewish women who are getting married in a Jewish ceremony, not precisely like the traditional kiddushin but with elements of it mixed with other themes.

"A lesbian wedding ceremony taking place in this large mainstream synagogue? Is this, too, a result of women rabbis?"

"In part. Not that women rabbis *necessarily* favor same-gender commitment ceremonies any more than male rabbis do. But the movement to accept both genders in similar professional roles was linked to the movement to accept differences in sexual orientation. Both were part of a revolution in people's thinking about the need for roles to be rigidly defined by gender. 'Both same-sex behavior and the equality of women disturb the traditional notion of what it means to be male and female.'[4] But now they are widely seen as part of the same shift in thinking that began around your era. *In the future, the existence of rabbis of both genders helps challenge compulsory heterosexuality.*"[5]

PUBLIC AND PRIVATE: *M'KDASH ME'AT* REVISITED

"Do more Jews come to the synagogue," we ask, "because of this greater inclusivity?"

"Yes. But not only because of that. There are Jews in the synagogue all day long. Come downstairs with me."

We enter a room that is filled with toddlers playing along with several adults. Next door are elderly people, spending the day with professional caregivers. "The full-service child-care and elder-care center (with creative interaction between the two) is routine now in synagogues. Other functions once performed by the mother in the home are now commonly supported by the synagogue community. For example, people often eat Shabbat meals together in the synagogue with a created extended family."

"Sounds like *m'kdash me'at* in reverse," I observe. Once the center of Judaism moved from temple to home with the family table replacing the altar. Now, what was once done by families in homes is moving back to the synagogue. But this shift worries me. "Children, aging parents, food, family...these were women's issues back in the bad old days. Now you're telling us that women rabbis are presiding as these become a focus for the synagogue. Isn't that another way of saying that women rabbis turned the rabbinate into women's work? Is that what feminism is supposed to accomplish?"

"I don't know about feminism," Yocheved confesses. "I'm just a woman from the Ancient Near East. All I can tell you is that after the external barriers to women's advancement began to crumble, many professional women (including women rabbis) found that there was still a glass ceiling far more difficult to confront than employer discrimination had been. Women found themselves struggling to balance love and work, the culture of the home and the culture of the work place, the competing expectations and values of two realms. They found themselves torn as they tried to protect their families from their work and their work from their families and to piece together a humane way to live a public and a private life. Women rabbis, because they understood the problem firsthand, helped to make the synagogue part of the solution.

"Women soon realized that entering the public sphere at the cost of abandoning the private one left traditional women's work, like child care, either undone or absorbed by public institutions.[6] The only way to avoid that was through massive restructuring of the work place and its values *and* massive support for the home and the values nurtured there. While that dream is far from realized, the synagogue has found an important role for itself as a mediating institution—not quite private and not quite public— that can support families by assisting in their functions and that also can affirm alternative values to those of the dominant work culture."

A synagogue is bigger and more diverse than a family but more inti-mate and family-like than most public institutions. It is an ideal commu-nity to help individuals span their various worlds. Women rabbis are now part of a greater movement of women who no longer are trying to "have it all" but rather are trying to find new ways to be true to their multiple callings by gaining support from their communities.

NEVER AGAIN

"What about relations with the non-Jewish world?" we ask. "Have women rabbis changed the way our Jews engage in interreligious dialogue, in community relations, in social activism?"

"That's a long story that's just beginning to be told," Yocheved says. "Women rabbis have been part of a transformation in the legacy of the Holocaust for Jews. Back in your day, Jews were still struggling with their history of victimization in an effort to move beyond anger, fear, self-pro-tectiveness and wrestle a blessing from the horror. Often they found them-selves mired in a particularism that grew—quite understandably—from a reluctance to let our unique suffering be forgotten by the world.

"Women rabbis became communal leaders and brought to this area their own perspective. They approached the issue of Jewish victimization as participants in another community of fate. As women, they shared a bond with women of every religion and race. They shared defining experiences linked to biology–menstruation, childbirth, nursing–experiences that are more constant across cultures than those that define male lives. They also shared a history of injustice: rape, sexual harassment, domestic violence, abuse, the constriction of all women's freedom by the awareness of the possibility of these crimes.

"Women helped the Jewish community to see its pain as a window into the pain of others. Women's empathy for other women, Jewish and non-Jewish, cracked open Jewish particularism and helped our community as it healed from its wounds and turned outward to the world."

The Tour Concludes

"The hour is growing late. Could you take us to see a Jewish federations office?" we ask.

Yocheved demurs. "We don't have time for that. But in the future they are models of cooperative institutions. There are no hierarchies whatsoever." At this point I detect that Yocheved may think that folks from the past will believe anything. It is time to end our journey.

We thank Yocheved and she disappears into the earth. Then we thank the witch of Endor and go on our way. I wake up with a start, a stiff neck, and a pang of regret. That was not the future! The Torah was right. The future cannot be seen, not even by someone conjured up by the witch of Endor. Suddenly, I feel excitement, even hope. The future cannot be seen for a good reason: *It has not been written yet.* I had to write this speech alone. But the real future? *That* we will all write together!

Notes

1. See Beverly Wildung Harrison, "a feminist moral theology is utopian, as all good theology is," in Carol Christ and Judith Plaskow, *Weaving the Visions* (San Francisco: Harper, 1989), 224.

2. Elizabeth Fox-Genovese, *Feminism without Illusions: A Critique of Individualism* (Chapel Hill: University of North Carolina Press, 1991).

3. See Joan Dash, *Summoned to Jerusalem: The Life of Henrietta Szold* (New York: Harper and Row, 1979), 76-77, for the tragic story of Szold's relationship with Ginzberg.

4. Judy Grahn, "A History of Lesbianism," in *Lesbian Poetry: An Anthology*, edited by Elly Bulkin and Joan Larkin (Watertown, Mass.: Persephone Press, n.d.), 70.

5. See Adrienne Rich, "Compulsory Heterosexuality and Lesbian Existence," *Signs: Journal of Women in Culture and Society* 5 (4) (Summer 1980): 631-90.

6. See Jean Bethke Elshtain, *Public Man, Private Woman* (Princeton: Princeton University Press, 1981).

Postscript

Sally J. Priesand

The end of our conference is fast approaching, and I hope you have found it as enriching, exciting, and energizing as I have. I certainly want to add my congratulations and thanks not only to the distinguished speakers whose insights have engaged and challenged us but also to those who have made this conference such a special time for looking backward and ahead. On occasions like this, I always dread being the last speaker. Everything that should be said has already been said and said so well, but I suppose there is a certain symbolism in allowing the first woman rabbi to have the last word.

Those of you who know me well or have heard me speak before know how much I believe in the value of empowerment, that the primary task of the rabbi is to help other Jews become more responsible for their own Jewishness. We accomplish this goal in a variety of ways: through education, through our own willingness to admit that we ourselves do not know everything and are still growing too, through hands-on activities that give those we serve an opportunity to do Judaism for themselves, through the example we set and the enthusiasm we display, whether in the religious school, at an adult education program, on the bimah, or even at a committee meeting, one that is called for a specific purpose or one that provides a forum for talking about the future and sharing our hopes and dreams.

We rabbis serve as role models in everything we do, and that is an awesome responsibility. If we are bored at services, then our congregants

117

will be bored. If we neglect to prepare properly for a sermon or a class, then people will stop coming to hear what we have to say. If we fail to teach Torah, day in and day out, then our people will never know the richness that is Torah. On the other hand, if we come to the bimah on Shabbat with joy in our hearts, then all who are present will begin to experience the sacredness of the seventh day, the day that is set apart from all others, a time for pause and renewal. If we seek always to find new insights in a Torah text, then we have the power to energize our people, to help them understand that every moment of our lives, from morning until night, has a Jewish component. And when we do that we not only enrich their lives and ours but we also ensure the survival of Judaism for future generations, not to mention the contribution we make toward the task of *tikkun olam*.

Everything we do sends a message. Let me tell you a story about something that happened in my congregation, something that I suspect has also happened in many of yours. A little boy was asked if, when he grew up, he might like to be a rabbi, and he responded: "Boys can't be rabbis; only girls can." I have been in my congregation for twelve years, and only recently did I realize that all the babies I have named have grown up believing that rabbis are women, unless of course their parents have made a conscious effort to take them to other synagogues where they see that men can also be rabbis. Twenty years ago, we would have rejoiced in the response of that little boy; today his response represents for us a challenge, a reminder that we send a message in everything we do. My very presence was interfering with that child's sense of empowerment.

Another story. In my congregation, during the Holy Days, members participate on the bimah. As we gathered together on the morning of Rosh Hashanah, preparing to enter the sanctuary, I suddenly noticed, much to my dismay, that all those invited to participate at this service were women. It was unintentional, had happened by accident, but I knew it was sure to engender comment on the part of the congregation. Some barely noticed, others thought it was wonderful, and still others expressed a feeling of discomfort. I empathized with this latter group because it reminded me of the discomfort I so often feel when I go to a Union of American Hebrew Congregations (UAHC) Biennial and Convention, and the enthusiasm I experience at being surrounded by three thousand Jews, men and women committed to the principles of Reform Judaism, is dashed when I look up at the dais and see a dozen men, leaders of our movement, both lay and professional, rarely a woman in sight. Everything we do sends a message, and actions speak louder than words.

That is not to imply that words are insignificant. One of the most important lessons I have learned these past twenty years is the power of language. Words have the ability to include or exclude, to hurt or to heal. Although they can be used for destructive purposes, to spread hatred and inflict cruelty, they also embody a spark of holiness. With them, we express love, create laughter, and learn to communicate. Words enrich, guide, educate, strengthen. They console and comfort, clarify and calm. They offer encouragement and spur us on to greater efforts.

Words also have the power to create images or destroy them. Recently, we inaugurated a new president of the United States. I found January 20 to be an exhilarating day. There was a sense of renewal in the air, the hope that this new administration would return to the United States its soul. Bill Clinton had been careful to emphasize the inclusiveness of his presidency. I admit to smiling when our new First Lady was introduced as Hillary Rodham Clinton; the use of her maiden name was yet another signal that the times they are a'changing. But when the Rev. Dr. Billy Graham offered the invocation, suddenly I felt excluded. This was to be a day for all Americans. Maya Angelou knew that; Billy Graham did not. Not only did he conclude his prayer with a Christian reference, but he began by addressing God as Father. For me, it was a powerful reminder of the images we create with our words, how everything we say has the power to include or exclude.

Twenty years ago we may have been able to excuse insensitive language. Today there can be no excuse, no overlooking the feeling of exclusion that words carelessly spoken so often bring. Everything we say sends a message, whether in the counseling we do, the articles we write, the sermons we preach, the liturgy we create, the classes we teach. Whenever we refer to the rabbi as he, rather than he or she, we set limits in the minds of women and men. Whenever we refer to God as He, ignoring the feminine characteristics of *Shechinah*, we create an image that interferes with every individual's right to imagine God in any way he or she finds meaningful. And whenever we create liturgy that contains only female imagery, we run the risk of destroying for some the ability to pray as part of our community. In my congregation, as in many, we have added the *Imahot* to the *Avot*. Personally, I like the change, but I am well aware that many do not, and many struggle with the words, particularly those who are guests at our synagogue.

There is, of course, another option. Instead of feeling the need to change every traditional Hebrew prayer, we could perhaps expend more effort in creating new prayers to supplement the ones that already exist, that hold for so many an emotional tie, a reminder of the links that bind the generations together. The *Avot* could remain the same; it could be followed by a new prayer celebrating the *Imahot*. That way we would not disenfranchise those who feel comfortable with traditional words, and we would also expand their horizons, offer to them a whole new opportunity for spiritual fulfillment. This could prove to be an important transitional step that will help create the change we seek ultimately to effect. The power of language can accomplish wonderful things. Today we celebrate that power; tomorrow we must expand it, but always with an eye toward sensitivity and balance, always with the hope of including rather than excluding.

Over the years, I know I have developed a reputation for saying what is on my mind without mincing words. On this occasion, I would be remiss in my responsibility if I did not do so, not for the purpose of making trouble, but with the hope of enabling future change. Emphasizing the positive is always satisfying, but ignoring the negative makes growth impossible. If we want to be honest with ourselves, then we must admit that the higher levels of leadership in the Reform movement do not reflect the changes that have taken place in our congregational life. Women are not nearly as well represented as they should be. Their underrepresentation is the greatest challenge we face as we embark now upon a third decade devoted to making real the principle of equality that lies at the heart of our movement. It is time to redeem the promise, and we can do that only if we are willing to admit that the percentage of change in the higher echelons of our movement has been minimal. We look at the faculty of HUC-JIR, at the boards that govern our major institutions, at the professional positions that provide leadership for Reform Jews, and we cannot help but echo the question that has already been asked: Where are the women?

The time for tokenism has passed. We must make a conscious effort to reflect in the higher levels of policymaking the reality that exists in the grassroots of our movement. Surely one of the most powerful lessons we have learned from the fight for civil rights in this country is that if you do not see someone who looks like you in a position of leadership, then you begin to feel left out; you have a sense that it cannot be done. We teach our daughters and our sons that everything is possible, there are no limits on what they can achieve when seeking to fulfill their creative potential and contribute to the vitality of Reform Judaism, but when they interact with the institutions in our movement, they discover a different message, a message that is all too prevalent in the larger society of which we are a part: a reluctance to believe that women are as competent and capable as men.

For twenty years I have listened carefully to the speeches that shape the character of our movement, to the resolutions that define who we are and what we believe and what we would like to be. The vision is there; the will to achieve it has sometimes faltered. If we want women to be on the faculty of HUC-JIR, then why do we not prepare those female students who show academic promise for these positions? Is that not how several of the men who serve our movement as scholars and teachers attained their positions? If we want women to be compensated equally and to have the opportunity to serve large congregations as senior rabbis, then why are we not out there as a movement educating our congregants, encouraging them to expand their horizons, and introducing them to the enormous creativity and sense of spirituality that female rabbis have already brought to Reform Judaism? I refuse to believe that a movement as vibrant and flourishing as ours cannot find the resources with which to redeem the pledge of twenty years ago. What I see happen all too often is the same thing that happens in our congregations: When confronted by criticism, people immediately become defensive and then are paralyzed to accomplish anything. There is no need to become defensive. Constructive criticism is not offered for the purpose of finding someone to blame but rather with the hope of moving forward together.

And that brings me to my final point. I hope our vision of the future will include a greater effort toward developing a true sense of family among all Reform Jews. I have been fortunate to have had many opportunities to celebrate the twentieth anniversary of my ordination, and I confess that I enjoyed every one of them, but one of the things that struck me most was how often we seem to work at cross-purposes with each other. As we have been reminded recently, historically the ball has often been passed from college to conference to union and back again, without a decision ever having been made and without an effort to bring all of us together.

I was delighted to see how many people chose to attend this conference, but I was greatly disappointed that the leaders of the Central Conference of American Rabbis and the UAHC are not here in large numbers to benefit and be enriched by the discussions that have taken place. I had expected them to be here because this is a moment we mark as a movement, a challenge that all of us face together. I had expected more men to be here, more members of the college faculty, more representation from the board of governors and the board of overseers of HUC-JIR, more students, rabbinic and cantorial, male and female.

Recently I delivered the Founders' Day address at the New York campus of HUC-JIR. On that occasion ten rabbis were honored for a quarter century of service to God and the Jewish people. What a wonderful milestone, not only in their lives but in the life of our movement. I remember wondering, where are the leaders of the conference and the union? Why are they not participating, together with the College-Institute, in this special and moving ceremony? I asked myself the same question when I attended ordination and noticed how sparse attendance seemed to be in comparison to previous years. Only later did I discover that the union was holding a meeting of its board of trustees that very same weekend somewhere in the Midwest.

These are events that should be celebrated together by all of us as one family. Each of the institutions of our movement is important, each has its own role to play, but all our lives would be enriched if we found more opportunities to work together toward our common goals, as families do, through word and deed, celebration and song. The days of hierarchy and power have gone, and a new time for networking and partnership has dawned. Change, for the sake of change, does not necessarily mean progress. The real test of progress is whether or not we are ready to recognize and respond to real needs, to reflect in the everyday activities of our movement the changes occurring all around us. If we are prepared to accept that challenge, then when we gather together to mark the twenty-fifth anniversary of this historic event, we will indeed have something to celebrate.

About the Authors _____ 🦋

HOWARD EILBERG-SCHWARTZ, Ph.D. is Associate Professor and Director of Jewish Studies at San Francisco State University. He received rabbinic ordination from the Jewish Theological Seminary in 1982. Dr. Eilberg-Schwartz's latest book is *God's Phallus and Other Problems for Men and Monotheism* (Beacon Press, 1994).

DAVID ELLENSON, Ph.D., is the I. H. and Anna Grancell Professor of Jewish Religious Thought at Hebrew Union College-Jewish Institute of Religion, Los Angeles. He received rabbinic ordination from HUC-JIR, New York, in 1977. Dr. Ellenson is the author of *Between Tradition and Culture: The Dialectics of Modern Jewish Religion and Identity* (Scholars Press, 1994).

ELYSE D. FRISHMAN is the rabbi of Congregation B'nai Jeshurun, the Nathan Barnert Memorial Temple in Franklin Lakes, New Jersey. She received rabbinic ordination from HUC-JIR, New York, in 1981. Rabbi Frishman is the author of *Haneirot Halalu: These Lights Are Holy* (Central Conference of American Rabbis, 1989).

NANCY FUCHS-KREIMER is Director of Religious Studies at Reconstructionist Rabbinical College, Wyncote, Pennsylvania. She is the author of *Our Share of Night, Our Share of Morning: Parenting as a Spiritual Journey* (Harper, 1996).

LAURA GELLER is Senior Rabbi of Temple Emanuel of Beverly Hills, California. She was ordained in 1976 at HUC-JIR, New York. She is the author of a chapter in *Four Centuries of Jewish Women's Spirituality: A Sourcebook*, edited by Ellen M. Umansky and Dianne Ashton. (Beacon, 1992), and she is a contributor to a volume entitled *On Being a Jewish Feminist*, edited by Susannah Heschel (Schocken, 1983).

ALFRED GOTTSCHALK, Ph.D., is Chancellor of HUC-JIR and Professor of Bible and Jewish Thought. He received rabbinic ordination from the College-Institute in 1957. Dr. Gottschalk's most recent publication is *Ahad Ha'am and the Jewish National Spirit* (Hasifriya Hatziyonit, 1992).

SALLY J. PRIESAND is rabbi of Monmouth Reform Temple in Tinton Falls, New Jersey. She received rabbinic ordination from HUC-JIR, Cincinnati, in 1972, and is a member of the Board of Governors of HUC-JIR and the Union of American Hebrew Congregations, representing the Central Conference of American Rabbis. She also chairs the CCAR committee on convention programs. Rabbi Priesand is the author of *Judaism and the New Woman* (Behrman House, 1975).

JONATHAN D. SARNA, Ph.D., is the Joseph H. and Belle R. Braun Professor of American Jewish History at Brandeis University. His most recent publication is, with Ellen Smith, *The Jews of Boston* (Northeastern University Press, 1995).

ELLEN M. UMANSKY, Ph.D., is the Carl and Dorothy Bennett Professor of Judaic Studies at Fairfield University, Fairfield, Connecticut. Among her recent publications is *Four Centuries of Jewish Women's Spirituality: A Sourcebook* (Beacon Press, 1992), which she coedited.

GARY P. ZOLA, Ph.D., is the National Dean of Admissions, Student Affairs, and Alumni Relations for HUC-JIR. He received rabbinic ordination from the College-Institute in 1982. Dr. Zola has edited several books and is the author of *Isaac Harby of Charleston: Jewish Reformer and Intellectual* (University of Alabama Press, 1994).

Index